~T

GO

~LIFE~

Dedication

To the One who has the good life in His heart; who makes it possible for us because of what His Son did; and who makes it actual to us because of what His Spirit continues to do.

Acknowledgements

My heartfelt gratitude is due to all those who by personal contact, book and tape have helped me to understand the good life; to my friend, Pam Kerr, who has so ably and enthusiastically typed and corrected the manuscript; to my colleague in the Gospel, Shirley Rothwell, who has maintained order and peace of mind in the office when the pressure is great; and as ever, to Anne, my wife, who has helped me to see the good life in practice and encouraged me to live that way.

THE GOOD LIFE

God's answer to our search for fulfilment

JIM GRAHAM

Marshall Pickering

Marshall Morgan and Scott
Marshall Pickering
3 Beggarwood Lane, Basingstoke, Hants RG23 7LP, UK

First published in 1987 by Marshall Morgan and Scott Publications Ltd
Part of the Marshall Pickering Holdings Group
A subsidiary of the Zondervan Corporation

British Library CIP Data

Graham, Jim
The good life.
1. Christian life
I. Title
248.4 BV4501.2

ISBN 0 551 01432 6

Text set in Bodoni Book by Brian Robinson, Buckingham
Printed in Great Britain by Anchor Brendon Ltd, Tiptree, Essex

~ Contents ~

1

The Good Life

His name was James. He was in his late eighties and had just had his leg amputated above the knee because of a circulation problem. I sat by his hospital bed, distressed that he was emotionally shattered and physically uncomfortable. The fine head seemed to have shrunk, the fresh complexion had lost its shine and had a strange pallor, the square shoulders seemed to droop even with more than half-a-dozen pillows to support them. The normally buoyant, optimistic spirit seemed to have been violated. As we talked on that warm afternoon in that large public ward in Glasgow Royal Infirmary, the weak old voice became animated once more. 'I've had a good life,' he said, 'and I have nothing to fear.' He was speaking of his past with satisfaction and of his future with secure anticipation. I knew him well – indeed I had known him as long as I could remember. Many times he had spoken to me of his boyhood and the years of his manhood. It had not been an easy life, nor had it been faultless, but it had been good. That was his verdict as he struggled with physical weakness and sensed that now perhaps life was drawing to a close for him.

Brought up the son of a farmer, when the order of the day was 'early to bed and early to rise'. Living on simple, ordinary food. Walking several miles to school each day as a boy; enjoying all the friendship and activity that village life provided in his young manhood – recalled often with a puckish, mischievous chuckle; working often through all of the daylight hours and finding great fulfilment in a job well done; finding some standing among his peers through his physical skill and expertise in farming matters; marrying and raising a family of four (one of whom was my mother) with very considerable pride; knowing disappointment and failure as well as fulfilment and success. He faced bereavement and financial stress with great honesty and courage. He had found reality in an uncomplicated relationship with God which stood the pressure of the years and remained intact when all was not well. Now was the time for appraisal of the past – all in all it had been a good life!

When he died a few weeks later I clearly remember wondering, what makes a good life? Is it robust health? Is it hard work? Is it good relationships – both intimate and more distant? Is it a simple life-style? Is it contentment with what you have? Is it the assurance that God is there and that He knows about you and loves you? Is it the conviction that death is not the end? Is it the security that accountability can be given without shame – even though judgment has sometimes been poor, blunders have been made, and faults have not been hard to find? Is it the confidence that the promises and provision of God will not fail – neither in life nor in death? In his case maybe it was many or all of these things.

All around us is the persuasion to believe that the good life is something which you can buy. If you purchase the right product, live in the right kind of house, wear the right kind of clothes, drive the right kind of car (with a sun roof, fuel injection, and a fifth gear!), go on the right kind of holiday, then you will be living the good life. While most of us at some level respond to this kind of invitation we know perfectly well that these things do not satisfy the deep inner urges of our hearts. Matter cannot satisfy spirit. We are fully aware that all these things are temporal; they rust, wear out, burn out, break, go out of fashion, become no more than a memory encapsulated in a photograph taken with the right kind of camera; and man has an incurable urge to be eternal. Material things make no contribution to immortality. Subconsciously we sense this. That is why materialism leaves us with an empty feeling. Man (whether he claims to be religious or not) is born an eternal creature, and lasting satisfaction and fulfilment come when we feel we are involved in something of lasting value. There is something in man which earth can never satisfy.

Furthermore, materialism does not satisfy because it is a severe master, and we are born to be free, not enslaved! So quickly we discover that the things we have worked for, saved for, sometimes schemed for and often dreamed to possess, eventually possess us if we are not careful. We discover we are married to a mortgage. We become slaves to gadgets and garments. After we have all our 'things' bought, delivered, and installed, and have enjoyed looking at them, touching them, using them, we find that they dominate, dictate and demand 'Press me, polish me, paint me, oil me, secure me, clean me, prime me, plaster me, repair me, take care of me'. So we can spend many years of our lives, and a great deal of our money, working for and serving things.

Not only do 'things' dominate us, but they beget monotony; and boredom is one of the major obstacles to the good life. 'Things' rapidly bore us. That's why styles have to change periodically – the design of kitchenware; the model of the car; the style of clothes. There has to be the long look, the short look, the baggy look, the crushed look, the bloated look, but there has to be a new look, always. So we have to re-upholster, replace, redecorate, or, at least, re-arrange the furniture. Each thing bores us. We get a certain amount of excitement shopping for it, looking for it, waiting for it to be delivered, putting it in just the right place, admiring it constantly for a day or two or three, having others notice it. Then suddenly days, weeks, months pass and we haven't even been conscious of this 'thing' for which we have worked, saved, planned so long and so hard. By then it is another new 'thing' which has to captivate us. 'Things' bore us because they are dead. They do not talk, laugh or love. And man has been born for fellowship. Even an argument is better than loneliness. No man is ultimately happy with things, because they don't satisfy his natural hunger and need for companionship.

Yet we continue to believe the persuaders (although we mock

them to ourselves and our friends and even write books denying them!) and many a marriage, many a family, many a reputation, many a healthy body has been sacrificed in response to them.

Others are convinced that the good life will follow when a coveted position is achieved. It may be in the company, in the organisation, in society, or even in the church. Then we believe that our personality can be expressed, our ambitions can find fulfilment, our authority can be exercised, and the things we have always hoped to see done can be accomplished. Subterfuge and humiliating conduct may accompany us on our route to the coveted position and we may hate ourselves for it, but pursue it we must and we will. More often, however, the goal is achieved by long hours, hard work, great loneliness, self-sacrifice and sub-consciously re-directing priorities. Unhappily many have testified that the satisfaction of arriving soon fades. When Benjamin Disraeli, twice Prime Minister of the United Kingdom, reviewed his life, he said: 'Youth is a mistake; manhood a struggle; old age a regret.' Hardly the good life! He may, of course, have been posing again, but those who could never be accused as poseurs have echoed his words.

Buzz Aldrin, the second man to step on to the moon's surface, suffered from mental depression and darkness in the years following his Apollo II moon mission. In his book *Return to Earth* he describes how he had spent most of his life competing for difficult goals. Ambition can be a good servant, but a hard and unfulfilling task-master. Its magnetic attraction can be as ethereal as the pot of gold at the end of the rainbow. Now with his moon walk – 'the most important goal of all' – behind him, he suffered from 'the melancholy of all things done'. These feelings of emptiness and meaninglessness are experienced by thousands who have achieved the goals they set themselves, and now have no further to go.

I saw him in the distance in a crowded supermarket one Saturday afternoon. He was too far away to make contact, but the sight of him awakened many pleasant and painful memories of the past. Then in the crowd he was gone. A good man, conscientious, hard-working, full of faith – in God and in what he was doing, honest, righteous, of unimpeachable integrity, meticulous in his attention to detail. He had built a company from very little to something significant, secured recognition within his own industry, gained high office and acclaim in the wider spheres of commerce and industry—and all that went along with these things. He had arrived, but with no wife to accompany him because his marriage had gone; no family to share his success because they were now scattered and uninterested in the 'empire' he had so carefully built for them and for others; no-one to share his lovely home and walk with him in his beautiful garden. Is this the good life?

Still others pursue pleasure as the means whereby the good life will be experienced. Its pursuit becomes a science with them. The art of life, as they conceive it, is to squeeze from every moment the utmost pleasure it will yield, but so often it turns to gall and bitterness at the last. Lord Byron may well be taken as typical of this conviction and way of life. He drifted, in the quest of pleasure, from one woman to another, and died an old man at the age of thirty-six, saying of himself on his last birthday:

My days are in the yellow leaf;
  The flowers and fruits of love are gone;
The worm, the canker and the grief
  Are mine alone!

His heart-breaking sadness and disillusionment are overwhelming.

Is the good life a delusion then? Are frustration and disappointment the inevitable consequence of seeking it? Most twentieth-century prophets are prophets of doom, not of hope—we need think only of George Orwell's *Nineteen Eighty-Four*, Aldous Huxley's *Brave New World*, Anthony Burgess' *A Clockwork Orange* and Nevil Shute's *On the Beach*. In the film based on the book *On the Beach* Mary cries, 'But there's got to be hope!' A nuclear war has wiped out civilisation in the northern hemisphere, and radioactive dust is drifting southwards, inexorably dealing out to all men radiation sickness, death and oblivion. The film records how Mary, her husband Peter, and others of their fellow-countrymen on the coast of Victoria in Australia live out these last doom-filled months before the end. One comforts herself with alcohol, others take reckless risks to win a motor race. Some pack as much pleasure-seeking into the time as they can. Others continue their daily routine as before, resigned to the inevitable. Open-air religious crusades hold the attention of thousands. For Mary's sake, Peter plants trees and buys a rustic garden seat in a charade of hope that somehow there will be a future for themselves and their baby, Jennifer. 'There's got to be hope.' Is this simply fiction and fantasy thinking in the light of the reality that stockpiles of nuclear powers contain explosives to the equivalent of more than 100 tons of TNT for each inhabitant of the earth? And recent developments in germ and chemical warfare make it feasible for poorer nations to destroy whole populations of other countries without going to the expense of producing nuclear weapons. There was a time when even irreligious man recognised that only God had the power to end the world. Now we have moved towards a point where almost anybody can do it.

Must we conclude, as Bertrand Russell did when he expressed his own view of the world in his poignant words: 'Only on the firm foundation of unyielding despair can the soul's habitation be safely built'? Is there no hope then? Must all man's seeking and longing always end in frustration at the last? Was Robert McNamara right when, as American Secretary of Defence in the late nineteen-sixties, he declared in a speech that 'all the evidence of history suggests that man is indeed a rational animal, but with a nearly infinite capacity for folly . . . he draws blueprints for Utopia, but never quite gets it built'. Is he right when, in the same speech, he also concludes that the nature of man himself is at the heart of the critical issues of our times?

At the turn of the century, before two world wars and the resultant cynicism contributed hugely to the breakdown of

Western civilisation which is going on all around us, where men are encouraged to suppress feelings of guilt and to laugh wrongdoing away, Lord Justice Cairns spoke with a workman who was an atheist:

> If you came to my house, you'd probably think it luxurious. You'd say that with all this I should be a happy man. I am – but my furniture and food have nothing to do with it. Every day I rise with the consciousness that God loves me and cares for me. He has forgiven all my sins for Christ's sake. And I look forward to the future with no dread . . . If I could be convinced that this is a delusion, my home would give me little repose, and my food would often lie untasted. It is a joy to me to tell you that the costly things in my home, which you cannot share with me, are not the things of which my happiness is made. Else I should wonder why they are given to so few. If tomorrow I left my house for a hovel, I would take my joy with me. It is Christ alone who satisfies.

The good life is not dependent on man and his achievements and failures. Nor is it dependent on where I live and whom I know. It is dependent on learning that there are rules for living and I need to keep them.

Some time ago we bought a microwave oven. It was virtually useless to us until we took time to read very carefully in detail the book on how to use it properly. When left to our own devices we could get it to work, but often it would spoil food rather than cook it. As with so many appliances, we need humbly to recognise that for best results we need to 'read the instructions of the maker'. Even after many months it is still necessary to check carefully from the book the time and degree of power required for a proper result.

So it is with life itself – we need rules for living which extend far beyond personal satisfaction, social convention and tribal custom. There needs to be an objective framework which applies in every age, at all times and for all people. God has already done this in giving us the Ten Commandments, which are probably the most relevant document we have because they are totally related to mankind's capacity to live and his yearning and insistent demand to make sense of life.

The key to the Ten Commandments is *respect.* The lonely supremacy and majesty of God is laid down and the sacredness of human life and the resultant right of the human personality are alike conserved. The inherent revelation of the Ten Commandments is that you cannot have one without the other. Reverence for God and respect for man must co-exist. No man can say that he loves and is related to God unless he also loves and respects his fellow man. Equally no man can really and truly love and respect his fellow man unless he sees that the true value of a man lies in the fact that he is a child of God. Without the manward look religion can become a remote and detached mysticism in which a man is concerned selfishly with his own soul and his own subjective vision of God and nothing more. Without the Godward look a society can become a place in which, as in a totalitarian state, men are looked on as things and not as persons. Reverence for God and respect for men can never be separated from each other. Circumstances may change; the situation may alter; what remains constant is the attitude of respect – for God and for man. This respect may well be expressed in different ways at different times, but the expression is always the expression of the same fundamental attitudes to God and man – an unchanging attitude with an infinite flexibility in the expression of it. Belief will always initiate and control behaviour. My belief about God and man will always be the reason for my behaviour towards God and man. This is an age of satire and ridicule, and *respect* needs to be reinstated.

Significantly these Ten Commandments are given to God's own people – God spoke and these were His words: 'I am the Lord your God who brought you out of Egypt, where you were slaves' (Exod 20:1, 2). A response to God's way to the good life requires a relationship to the living God. Therein lies an important principle: that the divine command is difficult to the point of impossibility without the divine dynamic. We are not looking here at a dull, formal, lifeless code of ethics, but rather a loving and grateful response out of a living relationship. This is the way to the good life.

The vast majority of Western society have debunked the Ten Commmandments as irrelevant today – perhaps subconsciously, but nevertheless really. Some have felt that they are *restrictive* – man doesn't need rules anymore. These are all right for the primitive, the naive and the inarticulate – but man has grown up now. He has become of age. This is the post-Christian era. Bishop John Robinson, for example, speaks of 'situation ethics' (there are no absolute standards – you decide each situation on its own merits, and so there are times when it is right to steal and murder, etc.) as 'the only ethic for man come of age'. What is needed now is liberty and freedom to express ourselves. It may well be true that scientifically, technologically and maybe even intellectually, man may have grown up, but spiritually and morally he is still desperately and patently immature.

In every sphere rules are needed – both for the sake of those involved and also to preserve the order and relevance of whatever it is we are involved in – whether it is playing a game or driving a car. Every car has its handbook with its clearly stated do's and don'ts. Driving on our roads is difficult and dangerous enough without getting involved in the nightmare of allowing everyone to do what they want at the speed they want without reference to the Highway Code. Clearly, in any civilised society there needs to be some restriction of our liberty if we are ever to enjoy and properly experience our liberty.

Others have felt that the Ten Commandments are *repressive.* True, some are positive, but most are negative, and negatives are bad psychology. To ban a book from publication is to make it a best-seller. 1962 was the only year that the Bible was not the best-seller in Britain in recent times. That was the year that D. H. Lawrence's *Lady Chatterley's Lover* went to the top. Censor a book or put an X certificate on a film and you will immediately stimulate many to read or watch what has been banned. Stolen fruit is sweet – such is the nature of man from the beginning.

However, if you are going to have morality you have to define not only what is right, but also what is wrong. Negatives are as necessary as positives. Bad psychology or not – this is the way of God – and this is the need of man. Even in the Garden of Eden there was a simple, clear, negative note. This was man in perfection. This was man before his racial fall. There can be no voluntary choice without a negative as well as a positive. Negatives are required if man is to be treated as a free being. This is where freedom lies.

Still others have concluded that at best the Ten Commandments can only ever be *relative*. There are times and circumstances when they are right, but equally there must be times and circumstances when they are wrong. For example, Claus von Stauffenberg was a devout Roman Catholic who plotted along with others to assassinate Adolf Hitler. They had come to the conclusion that Hitler was utterly evil and, for the sake of the future of Germany as well as the safety of a countless number of people, both Jew and Aryan, he must be eliminated. It is now history, of course, that the plot failed on the 20th July, 1944. The conspirators, including Stauffenberg, were executed. However understandable and laudable their intentions, were they right to contemplate and then to attempt Hitler's murder? The night before he set off with the fateful bomb to Hitler's headquarters, von Stauffenberg went to a church to pray. Did the circumstances set aside the Sixth Commandment 'Do not commit murder'?

A woman was taken prisoner by the Russians at the end of the Second World War. She was prevented from joining her husband and family in Germany. She understood that the only way she would be released and restored to them was by either becoming chronically sick or pregnant. With the help of an obliging guard she took the latter course. In due course she returned home with her baby to Germany to a rapturous welcome from her family who completely approved of what she had done. Was she right or wrong? Did her circumstances justify her breaking the Seventh Commandment 'Do not commit adultery'?

The fact of the matter is that the Commandments of God are never relative – they are always absolute. The Law of God is never 'on approval', so being left to us to decide whether we like it or not. The Ten Commandments are always right or always wrong in every situation. There is no such thing as a new morality – only an old immorality. The Commandments cannot be broken under the guise of love. In fact God defines love as the strongest motivation to keep the Commandments, not to break them. I need to be told what love would do since, when I am deeply involved emotionally in a situation, I am prone to allow love to become very subjective and so obscure the reality of the matter. I will find myself in a very confusing situation if my actions and reactions are governed by the relative question 'what does love suggest?' rather than by the absolute question 'what does God say?'

Once you have lost the absolute in morality, you have lost morality. If a thing is sometimes right and sometimes wrong it is not too long before you get to the place where the difference between right and wrong is blurred.

For many the Ten Commandments are *redundant.* After all they were given thousands of years ago. How can rules and principles produced for a society so different from ours and circumstances so completely removed from ours be relevant today? After all this is the age of Concorde, when it is possible to fly from Britain to the United States of America in under four hours. This is the era of moon-walking and space-travel.

We need to heed the simple, but observable, comment of Lord Eccles in *Halfway to Faith* when he says, 'The multitude of new facts and theories does not help us to behave better. Indeed, mankind as a whole tells more lies . . . It seems that because it is easier to travel to the moon, it is easier to make men unselfish and truthful.' However, although technological and scientific advances break exciting new ground; although clothes and fashions and language and customs change, neither human nor divine nature has changed. The passage of the centuries does not alter these. The need to control the one and reveal the other remains for ever the same.

In an age when there is a greater awareness of race than ever before, the Ten Commandments are seen to be applicable only to the Jews. They were given to them to be observed by them. Among the many divisions which have marked the development of the human race, that between Jew and Gentile has not been inconsiderable. Some Gentiles have even responded that, not only are they not Jews, but actually they are Christians and so the rules given to Jews have little or no relevance for them. After all Christians live in the New Testament rather than the Old Testament, and Christians have their own distinctive teaching. Jesus, however, was a Jew and He was born under the Law which is represented in the Ten Commandments. In any case nine out of the ten Commandments are repeated almost verbatim in the New Testament. In other words they apply to Christians as well as Jews. The fundamental responsibilities of the Christian are to love God and to love his neighbour as himself, and these instructions need to be clearly defined. The Ten Commandments do this with simplicity and disarming clarity. Did not Jesus say 'Remember that as long as heaven and earth last, not the least point nor the smallest detail of the Law will be done away with – not until the end of all things'? That appears to be comprehensive and conclusive enough. Jesus quite clearly states His intention that He did not come to abolish the Law, but to translate it and get it done. Therein lay the strength and effectiveness of His life and service.

Some have been concerned that to emphasise and ultimately to embrace the Ten Commandments would be to observe an unhealthy attitude towards *religion* (i.e. man's search after God) rather than to understand the reality of the Gospel (i.e. God's search after man). We are not under Law now, they argue, but under grace. We are not required any longer to live by a list of rules and regulations, but rather to recognise and receive the undeserved generosity of the heart of God.

However gloriously true this may be – and it is – we must beware that we are not adopting a cavalier attitude towards what God wants and what His will is. As Christians we affirm that it is not possible to get into a right relationship with God just by keeping the Ten Commandments, but God's Law still remains. What has changed is our motive for keeping the Law. Before Christ the motive for keeping the Law was to get right with God – and we failed abjectly. Since Jesus came we desire to keep the Law as an expression of our love and gratitude towards the One who has made it possible for us to enter into all that life is intended to mean and to be. In other words I no longer keep the Ten Commandments in order to get to heaven. I keep them because I know now assuredly that I am going there because of what God has so perfectly done for me in His Son Jesus. Love provides the *motive* for pleasing God whereas the Law provides the *means* for pleasing Him. The Law now becomes my *servant* rather than my *master*. God wants so much to make it clear to us and then to guide us into what *love* would do.

First, the Ten Commandments clearly *describe* the kind of being God is. He has high standards and wants the very best for His people. He certainly doesn't want to spoil your fun and fulfilment in life, but neither does He want *you* to spoil your fun and fulfilment in life. He gives these Commandments with the implicit desire for us that if we want to get the best out of life then here are His basic instructions for living the good life. The God and Father of our Lord Jesus Christ is forever a God of revelation – not a God of obscurity. There are basically two ways of gaining knowledge of the things which will not only frustrate your living the good life, but will also hurt you. You can get involved and make your own blunders and learn by experience all the pitfalls and hardships, or you can listen to someone else who knows not only what life is like, but knows what we are like. The Ten Commandments are God's cry to us to listen to Him.

Secondly the Ten Commandments give *direction* to us in living. There are two forms of guidance. There is *general* guidance and there is *particular* guidance. The Commandments give general guidance – they provide the framework and context in which particular guidance can be received. Many people have difficulty discerning particular guidance because they have never really come to accept God's framework of general guidance. If we are not prepared to keep in line with the *known* will of God it is unlikely that we will be able to find the *unknown* will of God for our lives.

Not only do the Commandments *describe* what God is like and give *directions* to us, but thirdly they *define* sin – the ultimate reason which frustrates us ever discovering and experiencing the good life. That twentieth-century prophet, Dr A. W. Tozer, makes a very shrewd comment when he says, 'To any casual observer of the religious scene today, two things will at once become evident: one, that there is very little sense of sin among the unsaved, and two, that the average professed Christian lives a life so worldly and careless that it is difficult to distinguish him from the unconverted man.'

You can never control, however, what you cannot measure. The Ten Commandments help us to measure sin – for sin is not just what the Sunday papers infer it is. As the spirit-level is to the carpenter, and the plumb-line is to the builder, and the thermometer and the stethoscope and the sphygmomanometer are to the doctor, so the Ten Commandments are to you and me. They enable us to know what we really are before God. As long as we compare ourselves with others, we may well feel very satisfied with ourselves. We need an objective test against which to measure our lives. The Commandments provide just such a test – not to make us feel guilty, but to diagnose the disease with a view to dealing with it.

Fourthly, the Ten Commandments prevent *deterioration* of goodness in both individual and corporate life. On the 15th October, 1975 following the party political conferences and preceding the new session in Parliament, Dr Donald Coggan, the Archbishop of Canterbury, issued a Call to the Nation. From his Lambeth home he called a press conference – with radio and TV present. He said,

> I want to speak not only to members of the Churches, but to all those who are concerned for the welfare of our nation at a

> time when many thoughtful people feel we are drifting towards chaos. Many are realising that a materialistic answer is no real answer at all. There are moral and spiritual issues at stake.
>
> The truth is that we in Britain are without anchors. We are drifting. A common enemy in two world wars drew us together in united action – and we defeated him. Another enemy is at the gates today, and we keep silence. We are afraid to speak out: it is time we spoke plainly.

There were five statements at the heart of the Archbishop's Call to the Nation.

1. Each man and woman matters.
2. The family matters.
3. Good work matters.
4. The other fellow matters.
5. Attitudes matter.

During the course of what he had to say, the Archbishop said quite positively,

> I believe the only creed that makes sense is:
> God first –
> Others next –
> Self last.
> I see this worked out in the person and teaching of Jesus Christ. He has shown us the way – He gives us the power to follow it. And this is where prayer comes in.

All in all what he was doing was presenting the substance of the Ten Commandments to the deteriorating nation. Letters began to arrive at Lambeth Palace by the sackful, so that after ten weeks the total was 27,000. It was a dramatic and very personal response from all sections of society: lord mayors, primary schoolchildren and sixth formers, families who did not go to church anymore, trade union branch secretaries. A nerve of the nation was exposed – a nation which recognised and feared decline and disintegration.

What our country needs is law-abiding citizens who obey not just human laws, but God's Laws. Our society deteriorates through lack of standards. The big issues which confront us are not first of all social, economic, environmental, racial or political, but moral and spiritual issues. What needs to be seen is not simply that the pound sterling is in constant danger of being devalued, but that people are in constant danger of being devalued – and all because of a society which by and large has debunked God.

As in the past, so now our society needs to re-affirm the Ten Commandments to prevent deterioration.

Finally, the Commandments *disclose* what pleases Jesus. The love that He spoke of was not always the kind of love that others understood. He was not speaking of a weak, fluctuating, variable sentimentality. He was speaking of a strong, resilient reality which operated in the realm of decision rather than emotion and had substance to it in that it was demonstrable in overt and observable ways.

On His last, urgent, memorable night on earth before He went to the Cross He said to His disciples, 'If you love Me you will obey My commandments'. He was referring to the substance of the Ten Commandments although His presentation of them was somewhat different. Jesus came not to get rid of the law, but to get it done and to enable people to do it too. He followed His insistence to His disciples that His love would be demonstrated by obedience (and in no other way) by promising, 'I will ask the Father and He will give you another Helper who will stay with you forever. He is the Spirit . . .'

So not only is what pleases Jesus disclosed, but the way and means to accomplish it is promised. The true disciple of Christ will look into His eyes and say, 'Your wish is my command, and your command is my wish.'

Such are the many and important functions which the Ten Commandments fulfil. We neglect and dismiss them at our peril, but we may embrace them with confidence and accept the dynamic of God to keep them with gratitude and so open up the exciting prospect of discovering something of the good life now in the midst of the years.

≈ 2 ≈

Choose the Right God

I love Oxford – its history; its atmosphere; its natural beauty – although I got lost there one night looking for St Edmund's College where I was to give some teaching on the Book of Daniel, and on another occasion I got trapped in a car park because the exit machine would not work properly. I often think of the generations of men and women who have gone there – kicking over the restraints of home and family life for the first time; feeling a great sense of academic achievement; wrestling with the basic, fundamental, insistent issues of life; asking and answering real questions; posing and solving real problems. From all over the world they come; from all over this nation they come, and there decisions are made and direction is found for the rest of their lives and the lives of others. It was there that C. S. Lewis – a typical twentieth-century agnostic, clever, cynical, contemptuous of puritanism, who, like so many of his contemporaries, regarded scepticism as an infallible mark of emancipation – became conscious of God in Christ, not as an interesting historical myth, but as a living reality. His whole life underwent a cataclysmic change, and the brilliance once used to confound Christian orthodoxy became employed in commending the Christian faith to doubting intellectuals. He tells his own story:

> Remember, I had always wanted, above all things, not to be 'interfered with'. I had wanted (mad wish) 'to call my soul my own'. I had been far more anxious to avoid suffering

than to achieve delight. I had always aimed at limited liabilities. The supernatural self had been to me, first, an illicit dram, and then, as by a drunkard's reaction, nauseous. . . . You must picture me alone in that room in Magdalen, night after night, feeling, whenever my mind lifted even for a second from my work, the steady, unrelenting approach of Him whom I so earnestly desired not to meet. That which I greatly feared had at last come upon me. In the Trinity Term of 1929 I gave in, and admitted that God was God, and knelt and prayed: perhaps, that night, the most dejected and reluctant convert in all England. I did not then see what is now the most shining and obvious thing; the Divine humility which will accept a convert even on such terms. The Prodigal Son at least walked home on his own feet. But who can duly adore that love which will open the high gates to a prodigal who is brought in kicking, struggling, resentful and darting his eyes in every direction for a chance of escape. The words *compelle intrare*, compel them to come in, have been so abused by wicked men that we shudder at them; but, properly understood, they plumb the depths of the Divine mercy. The hardness of God is kinder than the softness of men, and His compulsion is our liberation.

Such is the account of one man to whom God came – insistent, gracious, demanding. It is this God who comes to His creation with the startling, uncompromising imperative: 'I am the Lord your God who brought you out of Egypt, where you were slaves. Worship no God but me.'

That straightforward demand is born out of the divine love and concern for His creation. This command is inherently saying, 'You have a need and I insist that your need will be met not by fantasy or fallacy, but by reality'. The real problem of our time is an old problem: we worship the wrong God. Long ago Martin Luther said that man must have a god or an idol. Even the outspoken atheistic Voltaire observed, 'If there were no God it would be necessary to invent one'. Man is instinctively and incurably religious. His choice is not whether he will be religious or not, but what his religion is going to be. A man may not go to a place of worship or join with others who do. He may not say his prayers or read whatever holy book his peer group accepts. He may live his life convinced that he is getting on well without God – but in reality he is getting on quite well with another god – either recognised or otherwise. What air is to the lungs and food is to the stomach and knowledge is to the mind, God is to the soul. Man has always had a wide variety of gods. Bacchus, the ancient Greek god of wine, has his devotees to this day – and many become his obedient servants and sacrifice career, home, marriage, security and even life itself at his altar. Venus, the goddess of love, portrayed as having no hands or arms, is wildly revived in our sex-obsessed world of the twentieth century. Athena, the goddess of wisdom, has once more been elevated to glory in our contemporary society. Worship at her altar will bring vitality to a tired world and hope to a despairing culture. This view is as old as Plato, but it is widely held today. Bertrand Russell of Britain and John Dewey of America were among her most eloquent apostles. J. B. S. Haldane can see no limits to her possibilities. He actually argues that under her influence 'man will be able to think like Newton, to write like Racine, to paint like Van Eycks, to compose like Bach. They will be incapable of hatred as St Francis'. However, history and experience have shown that an educated man is not necessarily a good man. Sin can take on a high polish and speak with impeccable logic in the suavest of accents. It was not untutored savages, but the products of Western civilisation who were responsible for the last two wars – outstanding for their carnage in a century of blood.

Everybody has a god. This explains man's universal insecurity. Our Maker has deliberately permitted His children to feel innate insecurity that we might insistently and instinctively feel an inner tug towards Him as surely as the salmon feels the mysterious pull towards the place of his origin. In order to overcome this insecurity we have created false gods. They are sophisticated to match the sophistication of our time!

Today's unbelieving generation offers Self, supremely, as a god. The religion of this god is secularism – everything is seen from man's point of view, not from God's. Man's thoughts about God are made more important than God's thoughts about man. It is all part of the independent spirit of anarchy and lawlessness. It need not express itself in throwing petrol bombs at the police on the streets in the inner city or the border towns, or attempting to eliminate the Government by planting explosives in a Brighton hotel where they are staying during their party conference. It always expresses itself, however, in an insistence to do what I want regardless of God or anyone else. Secular humanism shapes its beliefs and behaviour by human reasons and social trends. The secular humanists' concept of God is reduced to what is fashionably acceptable. Supernatural religion is berated as something only for weaklings. Self-indulgence becomes the supreme sacrament and through clever manipulations of mental mechanisms of adjustment the educated heathen manages to convince himself that he is living the good life. He is amused at these evangelists who talk about sin, salvation, and a Saviour. The suggestion of final accountability and eternal judgment does not disturb him. However, starting from man, he is left with man. Tragically, what he gets does not satisfy the deeper longings of his soul. Instead of creating self-esteem, his self-indulgence only leads to a loss of self-respect. Pride gives way to shame. Success is followed by remorse and a hollow feeling of futility and cynicism. The god they want is not worth believing in. How often over these years, living and working as a pastor in commuter land outside London among some of the most delightful people I have ever met, have I confronted this plausible alternative to reality that the self is the god who can pacify the turbulent subconscious insecurities. It is not true!

The State is another god being offered to the twentieth century's insecure man. It bombards us with the propaganda that the State must play the role of god, feeding the hungry, caring for the ill, providing for every need from the cradle to the grave. In short, statism promises complete security from social dangers. It promises a great new age where the human ills which have blighted man will be eliminated by the State. The price, however, for this providential care is loss of human freedom. Man is asked to surrender true freedom in exchange for false security. Too often too late twentieth-century man has discovered that security without freedom is man's greatest insecurity—and man's most fundamental problems personally, nationally and internationally are far deeper than any government can handle. A present Utopia is consistently elusive and a future hope has no substance.

Science is yet another god for a progressively diminishing segment of society. The image of the man in the white coat in the clinically spotless laboratory is that of one who is omnipotent and omniscient for them. Pronouncements made by prominent scientists are received by some as authoritative. Towards the end of the twentieth century the great euphoria that characterised the early part of the century because of scientific brilliance and technological ingenuity has palled. Science and technology have created many more problems than they have solved. Whilst registering many positive gains they have also accelerated and accentuated many of the insecurities which have bedevilled man from the morning of time. The truth is that man's insecurities will never be fully removed by the test-tube technician—although from time to time man will be enormously impressed by the accomplishments and the confident pronouncements of science.

In the United Kingdom there remains a residual—even if subconscious—conviction that there is only one God. No matter which church you attended there was for many generations a tacit acknowledgment that there was only one God. The buildings in which the worshippers met differed vastly from one another; the forms of service sounded strange from one to the other; the natures and appearances of the leaders accentuated the differences—but always at heart there was the same God being worshipped. That fundamental monotheism has radically altered within a generation. The insurgence of other religions, mainly due to immigration, has profoundly changed that. The Muslim, the Sikh, the Hindu and the Buddhist in company with many others are among our fellow citizens. There are many supernatural gods in the United Kingdom today. A shrinking world caused by the intrusion of television into our living rooms, plus the easy availability and facility of international travel, has brought a whole new range of supernatural deities right into the centre of our lives. The cultures, philosophies and artistic representations of Eastern mysticism have all brought their own challenges to a wide variety of dimensions in our lives. The occult explosion with its ouija boards, seances, horoscopes, tarot cards, palmistry and a whole range of other expressions has certainly increased our awareness and experience of the supernatural, contrary to the reality of the God and Father of Jesus Christ. It has all happened so quickly and unexpectedly – and yet so plausibly and progressively – that we have hardly noticed the radical revolution which has taken place.

As well as the proliferation of supernatural gods there has remained the existence of natural gods. Sport, the garden, the house, the car, the business, the family, the girlfriend or boyfriend, the husband or the wife, or even the church have always had their place of deification within our society. These are the gods that we can see, hear, touch and handle.

We need to ask honestly the name of our god. Who is the last person or what is the last possession that you would like to lose? What is it that gives life purpose, meaning and fulfilment? On what do we spend our time, money, thought and energy most? What is it for which we would sacrifice comfort, friends, family and even honour sometimes? These are the questions which will lead us in due course to determine the name of our god.

Polytheism (the belief in many gods) is certainly not a thing of the past. We may ridicule those who believed and believe in a god of the sun, and a god of the moon, and a god of the sea, and a god of the sky, and a god of the fire, and a god of the wind, and a god of the river, and a god of the mountain, and a god of the wood. But the world – our world – is still crammed with gods and goddesses, both supernatural and natural, competing for the gifts, worship, devotion and commitment of men and women.

This First Commandment is saying: 'You have a need, and one way or another you will reach out to meet that need, and I want to be sure that you are not misled, duped or side-tracked, but that you would find reality. There are a multitude of ways to meet your need, but I want to impress upon you that there are no other gods apart from me'.

Because of the basic, fundamental nature of our need our recognition of and response to the one true God is the top priority. Man must have God, but not only must that God be the right one and the only one, but He requires to be at the centre rather than the circumference of our lives. He will not be tacked on as an optional extra like electrically-operated windows or a quadrophonic stereo system in a car. God says simply and clearly, 'If I am not first in your life I will not be second or third'. This is why many find it difficult to communicate with God and experience real, vibrant fellowship with Him – there is someone or something else in His place. It is not easy for us to recognise and experience this kind of total sovereignty and lordship since we have never had to come to terms with it in any other sphere of life. In the United Kingdom the sovereign is not really in control. Ultimate power does not lie in Buckingham Palace, but in Downing Street and the Palace of Westminster. The cabinet and the government elected by the people affect my life much more deeply and practically than does the sovereign. In this democracy I am free publicly and powerfully to criticise and disagree even with the government. I can register my personal antipathy with what is being said and done through the media and on the streets and ultimately register my antipathetic convictions at the ballot box.

Consequently this Commandment is not easy for most of us to embrace because of its absoluteness and total comprehensiveness. It is much easier for us to respond to the Ten Commandments as Ten Suggestions – to refuse or respond to as I like depending on my mood and my circumstances. The First Commandment is fundamental in this regard to all the others. Why should I – a modern Gentile European – give this absolute place and priority to the God of the Old Testament Scriptures? There are two reasons which God gave the Jews long ago and these two reasons remain intact for all men even today.

First of all because however accommodating and courteous and sensitive it may seem to be to others, there are no other gods. He is the only God there is. God precedes all the Commandments, but particularly this First Commandment, with the words: 'I am the Lord your God . . .' Literally He is saying: 'I am Jehovah . . .' i.e. 'I am I am . . .' No other God anywhere in history is called 'I am'. He is the only God who is. Every other god in history and experience is a fantasy god. However plausible, persuasive and practical he/it may seem to be, it is a fantasy god. It is not a god worthy of your worship, your devotion and your total commitment. It is heartbreaking not only to us as human beings, but to God to see the men and women He has created bowing down to gods who do not exist as gods in reality.

Admittedly it is much easier to come to terms with this in the case of *supernatural* gods. It is much more difficult in the case of *natural* gods (i.e. the family, the house, the hobby, etc.). Yet how tragic it is when a child is made a god. He becomes rebellious, resentful, damaged and unstable as a result. He certainly exists as a child, but not as a god. The same tragedy exists in the case of making a garden a god. It may be an award-winning garden – fragrant, wonderfully attractive and beautifully ordered, but it remains a garden not a god. One day, as circumstances change, it will become overgrown, covered in weeds, and a heartbreak to remember what it used to be like 'in the old days'. So also when a house is made a god. I remember the grief of a visitor from the United States returning to the United Kingdom for the first time in forty years to see the place where so many childhood memories were born and to share it now with his partner of the years, only to discover that it had disappeared out of sight and certainly beyond recognition under the developers' vision and genius. You can never call child, garden or house 'I am'. There will come a day when we will have to say of all three 'it was'. You are going to have to survive and continue life without them. But God in His mercy and love cries with insistent concern 'Worship no God, but me. For I am real – I exist!'

Michel Quoist expresses the bewildered desire and demand of many:

> Lord, do you hear me? . . .
> Lord, I can no longer find my own door.
> I grope around blindly,
> I knock against my own walls, my own boundaries,
> I hurt myself,
> I am in pain . . .
> Lord, Lord, do you hear me?
> Lord, show me my door, take me by the hand,
> Open the door,
> Show me the way,
> The path leading to joy, to light.
> But, Lord, do you hear me?

Behind this prayer is the uncertainty – maybe even the fundamental fear – that God is not there. The fear that it is all fantasy, nothingness, empty hopes, and wishful thinking. It is in answer to this questing uncertainty that the terse, straightforward simplicity of 'Worship no God but me' comes with reassurance.

The other reason why this First Commandment was given is because the God and Father of our Lord Jesus Christ sets you free. Every other god at some level, and in some way, will enslave you. 'I am the Lord your God who brought you out of Egypt, where you were slaves.' I want you to be free. Do not go back into slavery. Worship me alone. Herein lies your hope and experience of liberty.

One of my prize possessions is a book by Fred Lemon called *Breakout*. Fred has written on the fly-leaf: 'To Jim, the Past is under the Blood. The Present is under the promises. The Future is in His hands. Fred Lemon. 1 Corinthians 1:27–31.' I met Fred years ago and was captivated by his spirit. He tells in his book how it was very quiet in his cell after the warder had escorted him back from the 'dungeons' – the punishment cells. He tells how he threw himself on the hard bed, a black bitterness of soul filling him. He vowed to himself that on the next day he would get hold of the sharpest knife in the mail-bag room – and murder would be done. Weary and tormented he pulled the coarse blanket round his shoulders and closed his eyes. The events of that night can only be described by Fred himself. Dramatically and unexpectedly God met him, and Fred Lemon, a confirmed and violent criminal, on the eve of attempting to break out of Dartmoor Prison, unexpectedly broke out spiritually, and found freedom far greater than that of the open moor – even though he remained a prisoner. So it has been for a countless number down through the years – recognition of and response to the God of the Bible has brought freedom.

Polytheism will forever be unsatisfactory because it will never give security, and security is the firm base on which freedom is built. I never know where I am when there are many gods clamouring for my attention and devotion. Is there a vengeful god who is paying attention to me whom I have failed to satisfy? Is there a god somewhere whom I am unaware of – how can I respond to such a god if I do not even know of his existence? This leads to great vulnerability and moral disorder. There are those who are quick to capitalise on this kind of confusion. The priest, the guru, the holy man, the witch-doctor are all willing to place a pattern on the chaos which ensues. Since they are 'in the know' they can easily and firmly bring the unsuspecting worshipper under their control for their own benefit. It is easy to manipulate those who come to these sources for the assurance of reality – and many do. It is so refreshing and stabilising to hear the God and Father of our Lord Jesus Christ say so categorically (as He does in this First Commandment) 'I alone am real!'

Not only does polytheism fail to bring security, but it also fails to bring an awareness of responsibility which again is indispensable to true freedom. With a multiplicity of gods around me I can never know to whom or to what I owe my allegiance. I cannot satisfactorily answer the question 'to whom shall I commit myself?' because I am unable to discern to whom I am ultimately answerable. There is a mistaken concept of freedom which abounds within our culture. Freedom is doing whatever you want. This in fact is the ultimate bondage. William Wordsworth has given classical expression to this in his 'Ode to Duty':

Me this unchartered freedom tires
I feel the weight of chance-desires;
My hopes no more must change their name,
I long for a repose that ever is the same.

This may not seem so on the surface, but when we come to terms with the true needs of our nature 'in the quietness of thought' as Wordsworth puts it, 'I supplicate for Thy control'. As I remember my own school days the masters and teachers whom I appreciated most of all were those who exercised a fair, consistent and clear control in the classroom. The only healthy and happy homes in the land are those where a wise and loving discipline exists. During military service the recruit may well grumble and grouse at the rigours and apparent irrelevance of training, but he infinitely prefers an iron discipline to laxity and indirection. Someone has said that 'a man's real difficulties begin when he is free to do what he likes'. The prodigal son (Luke 15) was in this condition, but in the end he preferred the lot of one of his father's hired servants to the free life he had followed in 'the far country'. The people of Israel, in the day of the prophet Samuel, grew weary of an invisible monarchy, and demanded from him a visible king who would lead them in conquest and lay down rules for common social action.

Man's true life consists, not in the things he possesses, but in the things that possess him. It is not the things that belong to us that set the bells of our nature ringing, but the things to which we belong – the attachments that bind us, the loves that grip us, the interests that govern us, the appreciations which inflame us, the aspirations which lift us, the causes we serve which command our allegiance, and engage all our powers. All of this is recognised in the First Commandment.

We need a controlling power which will recognise the strength of our passions and appetites and the potential of our abilities and opportunities and belt them to useful ends. The first essential for power of any kind is rigid and constant control – whether it is the power of the atom, the fire, the wind, water or electricity. All high-powered machinery has its controls – whether it be the computerised mystery of Concorde; the multitude of those on the ground with their bewildering collection of screens, charts and panels at the space-centre; or simply the gears and brakes of the motorcar. Even more urgently does the delicate, complicated, high-geared machinery of the human personality demand its controls. The Old Testament prototype of physical strength was Samson. Yet the tragedy was that he lived a masterless life, when he badly needed a master. In the end John Milton puts into his lips the tragic consequences of a life which had neither control nor accountability:

> I, like a foolish pilot, have shipwrecked
> My vessel trusted to me from above
> Gloriously rigged.

Human nature without adequate control is in a state of perpetual siege. Civil war rages in its members. Without control we are like a team of wild horses stampeding in opposite directions at one and the same time; like a ship's crew in mutiny against the captain; like the members of an orchestra playing from different musical scores; like an army that disobeys orders and ignores king's or queen's regulations. We need a strong hand on the reins, a captain on the bridge, a maestro who can wield a baton, a commander who enforces obedience. Then, and only then, have we found true freedom.

This is God's purpose in giving this very first Commandment – to bring us not only into reality, but also into freedom. When God is first and is truly worshipped as such then you can enjoy your children, and your garden, and your house, and whatever else, to the full without being a slave to any of them.

Long ago when the Huguenots were besieged at St Quentin, the Spaniards shot an arrow into the market place, carrying a scornful demand for surrender. Coligny, the commander of the Huguenots, shot back the paper, adding only two words, 'Regem habemus': 'We have a King'. The one to whom we give our allegiance, homage, devotion and commitment will determine the way that we live our lives. If a man worships a licentious god like the Baals he will become a licentious man. If he worships a hard stern god, then he will, as the world has so often tragically seen, become a hard, stern, inflexible man. If he worships a sentimentalised god of his dreamy wishful thinking, he will have a sentimentalised idea of religion. If he worships a God who has revealed and declared Himself in truth and reality, then his life will manifest that unclouded openness and liberty. It is from here that ethics makes its beginning. It is here that the good life starts. A man's god dictates a man's conduct, consciously or unconsciously.

The Christian believes in the God who is not only the God and Father of our Lord Jesus Christ, but who actually has become incarnate in His Son. He is the God whose mind and heart and character is in the life, death and resurrection of Jesus. For that very reason the good life is the life of Jesus being lived out in us by the power of the Holy Spirit.

3

Rivalry is not tolerated

We become what we worship. Generally this is not an accepted conclusion, but that neither minimises nor denies the truth and reality of it. Worship is considered to be restricted to religious buildings and liturgies, when in fact it lies centrally at the heart of life itself. The way we live is deeply and fundamentally affected by who and what and how we worship. Our ignorance of what affects our lives most deeply and our disregard of the true nature of worship, carry their own severe penalties. The Second Commandment is an insistent demand by God that we confront the reality of worship which lies at the centre of every man's life. The First Commandment is concerned with *whom* we worship (i.e. that we worship the right God), while the Second Commandment is concerned with *how* we worship (i.e. that we worship the right God in the right way).

Worship is all about an attitude that is the consequence of a relationship rather than an activity that specifically engages us. We can be concerned with, and even discuss and disagree about, the activity of worship and miss the whole point of it as a result. Instruments are important in worshipping God, but worship is not really about organs or pianos, tambourines or guitars, drums or trumpets. We may well need to spend more time considering the content of worship, but in its essence worship is not about hymns or choruses, anthems or vespers, spontaneity or structure, liturgy or liberty, freedom or form. Worship in reality is about us and God, and how real or otherwise that relationship is. Perhaps the most comprehensive and best-known definition of worship comes from the late Archbishop William Temple:

> Worship is the submission of all our nature to God. It is the quickening of conscience by His holiness; the nourishment of mind with His truth; the purifying of imagination by His beauty; the opening of the heart to His love; the surrender of will to His purpose – and all is gathered up in adoration, the most selfless emotion of which our nature is capable.

Worship is about *whom* we worship and *how* we respond to that. The big question is 'Whom are we bowing down to?' (Exod 20:5). That is not simply a conceptual, theoretical, theological question. It is a very physical, practical, tangible question. We have often spiritualised what God wants us to embody. Our attitude is fundamental, but that will determine our activity.

That is why Paul insists, as he explains the implication of the gospel in the first eleven chapters of Romans, that there must be a consequence to that. Chapter Twelve of Romans begins 'So then . . .' i.e. as a result of all I have explained – complicated and difficult as you may have found it – there needs to be a practical, physical and obvious response. 'I appeal to you: offer yourselves as a living sacrifice (literally: *ta somata humon thusian zosan hagian* – 'your bodies a living, holy sacrifice') to God, dedicated to His service and pleasing to Him. This is the true worship that you should offer.' Chapters One to Eleven of Romans deal with soul and spirit, but Chapter Twelve deals with body and mind (Rom 12:1, 2) – the outward expression and the inward experience that result from recognising who God is, and responding to what God has done and wants to do.

Clearly from the Second Commandment God wants all of you. This is the emphasis, too, in Paul's letter to the Romans. I remember so clearly the morning I learned of the death of one of my dearest and most respected friends. His name was

Len Moules. Len had been a missionary on the Nepal border, then Field Leader, then British and ultimately Overseas Director of the Worldwide Evangelisation Crusade for forty years. He came to our church and, on his retirement from WEC, he came to live across the road from where we live. Inevitably, he became part of the leadership of our church and eventually joined the pastoral team. The morning of his Homecall will forever be unforgettable so far as I am concerned. Some of these details are almost too personal to share. One of the events of that morning involved me in phoning a London hospital. In the full flush of his busy, demanding and energetic life, Len had decided to donate his body to medical research. I had to contact this hospital as a result. I must have waited for about two hours for a reply from the hospital. When it came, I was informed that they would not require his body. Even on that morning it impressed me that in death his body was not required, while certainly in life it was – by God. God is on the lookout for bodies that will recognise Him and then respond to Him and allow Him to express His life.

In the Old Testament, if you wanted to worship God you had to bring a body with you – often that was considered to be a dead body. After all, in the Temple the worshipper was required to slaughter his own lamb by slitting its throat, so making the sacrifice his own. The blood was caught in a gold or silver bowl, and passed to a priest who was at the end of a long line of priests which led directly to the altar. The bowl was passed along the line until it reached the altar where the contents were dashed. The slain lamb was then taken and roasted – never boiled, since nothing must touch it; not even the sides of a pot. It was roasted over an open fire on a spit made of pomegranate wood. However, quite clearly in the Old Testament, as well as the New Testament, what God was really looking for was not so much a dead body as a living body. Christianity certainly concerns itself with bodies – living bodies. There is a great deal in the Christian gospel about bodies – it speaks about the *resurrection* of the body and the *redemption* of the body. Of course, the very heart of the gospel is that God became *incarnate* in a body like ours. What we do with our bodies, then, is of great importance to God. He will never take our body by force. Hence Paul's appeal to '*offer* yourselves . . .' (Rom 12:1). The tense of that verb is significant in that it means 'once and for all'. In other words our giving of ourselves to God is to be complete and final and permanent. How significant this is for the Second Commandment – not only that we recognise the right person to whom we will give our homage, commitment and worship, but that we will do it in the right way.

In 1928, writing to the Conference of Church of England Clergy, Evelyn Underhill wrote:

> We are drifting towards a religion which, consciously or unconsciously, keeps its eye on humanity rather than deity – a religion which lays all the stress on service and hardly any on awe.

The Second Commandment, as well as the First, is a powerful reminder that we need to get the balance right. It is significant that, on the day of Pentecost (Acts 2), the first consequence of the Holy Spirit coming upon the people of God in power and fullness, is that they recognised and declared who God is and what He is like and then poured out their hearts in worship. The first direct effect of Pentecost was worship. Having got this in its true perspective, and in its proper priority, so many other effects were unmistakably seen and the world (or the Church) was never the same again. It is certainly not without significance that the first part of the Ten Commandments insists on our attitude to and acknowledgment of God, and the second part then deals with our relationship with and respect for our fellow human beings.

Of all the Commandments, many feel safest and least threatened by this one. With a clear conscience many can say, 'I have never worshipped a statue, or a picture, or an emblem. Whatever other Commandments cause me to pause and consider my personal position, this one does not affect me'.

In the seventeenth century this Second Commandment was taken so literally that many Christians felt that any form of art was forbidden for them, and had to be eliminated from their personal, social, domestic and religious life. Puritan homes, for example, were bare and austere and precisely functional. Little comfort was provided for fear of limiting spirituality, and little beauty existed in case admiration should detract from a Godward worship. Of course religious buildings did not escape the powerful religious convictions which were born. Many churches and cathedrals were desecrated, and some priceless treasures were completely and wantonly destroyed with hammers and axes. This phase and emphasis has left its mark even on contemporary Christianity. The creative arts have become largely ignored by Christians, and they have left these formative expressions of reality, which are born in the soul and spirit of man, to people who do not know how to use them to the glory of God. This has produced a powerful and destructive harvest. The devil is not slow to utilise what does not belong to him, but has been abandoned to him by wrong attitudes which stem from a wrong understanding of God.

God reveals Himself to be intensely interested in beauty as well as in goodness and truth. Since He has created us in His own image and after His own likeness, then we are to be creators of beauty too. We need to recapture the reality that form and music and colour bring deep delight to Him as well as to us. Disorder and discord and drabness are as unacceptable and unpleasant to Him as they are to us. He certainly created the world before He created us, so that there would be a suitable place for the men and women of His creation to live. But the world which He created is an expression of His true nature and character and a delight to His eyes. Did He not say, when He looked upon what He had done in the beginning, 'This is good; this is very good'? Man can be so smugly conceited when it comes to created things that he insists that it is all for him – it is not so. The world as He created it was a pleasure and delight in the first instance to God.

Man's conceitedness has always been in danger of blinding him to the truth. Copernicus, in 1543, published his famous *De Revolutionibus Orbium* in which he claimed that the earth, far from remaining motionless at the centre of the universe, actually travelled round the sun. The full implications of this theory were not grasped at first, but from the start it became crystal clear that this little planet, on which we mortals dwell, was robbed of its position of unique and unrivalled importance. Men were so startled and upset by his clearly declared and substantiated conclusions that in their irrational way they accused him of atheism and blasphemy. Such is the deeply ingrained conceit of man that he hits out – even in ignorance – at anything which destroys his concept of his central position.

So often when we design and decorate a church building we are only concerned about what people want and how people will think about it – how many fruitless and contentious man-hours have been spent on that! We seldom take the time and trouble to consider what God would like. He was concerned to share with King Solomon, in some considerable detail, how He wanted the Temple built and furnished. Embroidery, form, size, sculpture, woodcarving and other plastic arts all have their place there – coming from the heart of God and giving pleasure to Him (1 Kgs). He is interested in where His people meet and what they do there. How important it is that we recognise and give room to creativity which is a direct evidence of the one who created us.

The problems with which God has struggled in the hearts and conduct of His people are insubordination, immorality and idolatry. These have been God's concern right from the beginning. All three have brought untold misery and frustration right from the very beginning. It is with the last – idolatry – that this Commandment deals. The details and circumstances have changed through the generations, but the problem remains the same. Idolatry is not an antiquarian relic of the past, nor is it confined to a less progressive culture than ours. It is a present threat and in essence embraces two confusing errors.

First of all, idolatry involves allowing the means to become the end. In its simplest form an idol was, and is, a means towards making memory and worship easier. However, in the end it became itself the object of worship. The means had become the end. This has constantly happened in the Church. A liturgy is a means of worshipping God; but a fixed liturgy can become an end in itself, so that the means and the method of worship can become more important than the worship itself. This is true not only of written liturgies, but also of unwritten liturgies which are often regarded as spontaneous and extempore. The form and content and execution of worship become the focal point rather than the One to whom it points and leads. In the same way a system of Church government is a means towards the welfare of the Church to enable corporate life to function decently and in order. But a system of Church government can and does become an end in itself, so that people end up by being more concerned about the way the Church is governed than with the Church itself—its life, health, function, relevance and effectiveness in the hands of the One who died for it and who desires to express His life and power through it. A church building is a means whereby a group of people can worship God; but people strangely end up by worshipping the building itself, and so become more concerned about the place where worship is offered and fellowship is experienced, than with the reality of the worship and fellowship expressed there. Whenever means become ends then idolatry exists as really and as destructively and as threateningly as ever it did.

Secondly, and perhaps more obviously, idolatry occurs when we substitute the thing for the person—the dead idol has taken the place of the living God. This is constantly happening in life generally. In the days of the Industrial Revolution, when the effectiveness and efficiency of the machine were discovered, the fatal mistake—from which industrial relationships have not even yet recovered as this micro-chip society has so clearly demonstrated – was that the machine was regarded as more important than the person. Men, women and even little children were regarded as no more than machine-minders, hands to be used to keep the machines going and the profits rising. People were used as things, and it takes a long, long time to undo the damage that using persons as things, and regarding people as hands, can do to the relationship between employer and employee.

In the same way, this worship of the thing created by man can invade the home. I have never been interested in, nor addicted to, crossword puzzles. They have always seemed to me a fruitless pursuit accompanied by all kinds of mental anguish. I believe that once, however, a crossword puzzle had a clue in it, 'What makes a home?' The required answer was nine across with two U's in it – 'furniture'. Incidentally, that is precisely what does not make a home, as many have discovered to their great cost, and yet that is precisely what so many give their time, energy, creativity and money to, as they give themselves to building a home. A home will always be people, family, and tender, but strong and resilient, relationships. I well remember the early morning when I realised that our home had become a house. I had come from the Western Infirmary in Glasgow, where I had watched my mother slowly die. She had been the one who stood at the centre of our family relationships, and with her gone our family life significantly disintegrated. I was to live on in that house for some considerable time afterwards, often on my own, but it was never the same again – it was just that, a house, not a home any longer although the carpets, curtains and furniture remained the same.

We do well to examine our life-style to see if one of the strong characteristics of idolatry is not present in our lives generally because we have given things – the objects of man's creativity – first place in our lives rather than people. Idolatry is by no means dead. Idolatry is not the ridiculous mistake of primitive people. Whenever means become ends, and whenever things become more important than people, and whenever anything (or indeed anyone) usurps the place that God should have, idolatry is still powerfully and unmistakably there.

The implications, then, of this Second Commandment are not difficult to see. There are three kinds of images that we build which subtly and often quite quickly take the place of God. First of all, and perhaps easiest to appreciate, there are *material* images. Why, anyway, would anyone want an image? The fact of the matter is that most people think in pictures rather than in words. The preacher or the teacher or the speaker who can paint pictures with words will always be more acceptable and effective than the one who can't. In fact this whole process has crept into our language, since we respond to something we have heard and understood by saying, 'Oh, I see!', 'I understand!', 'I've grasped and appreciated what you are telling me!' Visual aids are common, not only in the classroom, but also in the church. Jesus, of course, was the master-teacher and He frequently appealed to the eye-gate as well as the ear-gate. He would speak simple, yet profound, truth by referring to incidents and objects which were part of the common life of those to whom He was speaking. Most of us have real difficulty when it comes to thinking abstractly in words only. When I say 'uncle', 'tube-train', 'butter', 'seaside', 'aeroplane' you will immediately have a picture in your mind. You will immediately draw on your experience and encounters and understanding of all these things, and have a picture in your mind. It may not be an accurate picture of what is in the mind of the person who is speaking to you, but it is a picture. When I say 'love', 'patience', 'courage', 'joy' it gets much more difficult, but again your mind will struggle through to invest these concepts with people and personal experiences or remembered events. When I say 'God' – what kind of picture does that have in your mind? No one has ever seen God. Moses wanted to, but God refused to allow that to happen. But this is fundamentally the reason why people want an image. Generally, we find it difficult to worship, trust, rely on and be involved with someone when we cannot see Him. As we have seen, God is concerned in the First Commandment that our need is met, but that it will always be the right and the real God. The Second Commandment is an expression of God's concern, not only that we will worship Him in the right way, but that in our humanity we have a need to see what we are trusting. The Second Commandment was given, not to those who worshipped pagan gods, but to those who wanted to worship Jehovah – the God and Father of our Lord Jesus Christ. We have a phrase in our language which doesn't quite convey reality – 'seeing is believing'. That is not so! It would be more accurate to say, 'not seeing is believing' or 'seeing is not believing'.

After all, when I can see something I no longer need to believe to make it real. For example, if I have faith that God will provide £50 for me tomorrow, at that point of believing I do not have that £50 in my hand. I do not need faith if I already have a cheque for that amount on my desk with my name on it.

Here is the problem that we face more often than not – to believe someone or something which we have not seen and, in the case of God, cannot adequately imagine. The foundational tenet of the Christian, and indeed of the Jewish, faith is that God is *spiritual* (read Ps 139:1–18). He does not need to assume any material, visible or corporeal form for His existence. Secondly, God is *eternal* (read Isa 57:15). He is independent of time and space and lives outside them, rather like an author lives outside the people and the events of his book. Thirdly, God is *moral* (read Mic 6:8). He is intensely concerned with the way we react, respond and behave. He wants us to be like Himself – holy and good – and for this reason we were created 'in His own image'. Our tendency is to try to make God like man, whereas God's insistence is to achieve the exactly opposite result. Holiness and goodness, however, are very difficult concepts to grasp apart from representing them somehow. Fourthly, God is *personal* (read Ps 103:13, 14). He is interested in us and cares for us and provides for us like a father. When these four characteristics, which are fundamental to our understanding of God, are all put together we have a problem which gives rise to the tendency to create an image.

The fundamental principle of an image is that you picture something in terms of what you have already seen and recognised. You always work from the known to the unknown. If you are going to have a visual image of God, you will start with something which you already know on the face of the earth, in the depths of the sea, or in the limitless reaches of the sky. So the lion speaks of God's strength, the sun speaks of God's favour, and the eagle speaks of God's wisdom. In other words, if you are going to have a visual image of God, you start with something which He Himself has made. That is exactly what the Second Commandment is about.

Why is this so wrong? Why is this so clearly and strictly forbidden? Basically for three very important reasons. First of all, it reduces God in *size*. When you do this you turn the Creator into the creature or the thing which He has made – no matter how splendid and impressive and awe-inspiring it may be. By doing this you bring God down to a place, and into your possession, where you can *control* Him. God can so quickly be reduced to the level of a mascot, even though the mascot receives a place of prominence and even reverence in the home or the church. This causes Isaiah to cry out in frustrated inability, 'To whom can God be compared? How can you describe what He is like?' (Isa 40:18–31). He goes on to speak of Israel's incomparable God – there is nothing, however fine, in creation to which you can compare Him. It is rather like translating Shakespeare into a very primitive language which has a simple and very limited vocabulary. Something of the beauty and the poetry of the original has gone and you are left with something incomplete and ordinary no matter how you try. It is not surprising that those who speak that language would find it difficult to understand how English-speaking people could ever be so enamoured with the works of Shakespeare. It is rather like playing Beethoven's Ninth Symphony on a comb and paper. Something of the melody may be vaguely reproduced, but the grandeur and the depth and the magnificence require the strings and the brass, the wind instruments and the percussion of a fine orchestra moulded together by a gifted and able conductor.

Secondly, it restricts God in *activity*. From being the God who is everywhere, He becomes the God who is here – localised, resident and immovable unless I choose to move Him somewhere else. So God who is in reality beyond time and space, becomes localised within time and space. This, of course, is much more conducive to our natural understanding and imagination, for conceiving someone who is everywhere all the time in every generation is beyond us because it contradicts our experience. We can grasp, much more easily, a God who doesn't move, walk, talk or respond to us. The implication of this, however, is profound – there is only a one-way relationship with Him. He can no longer take the initiative and move towards us – it must always be we who take the initiative and move towards Him. Therein lies one of the most fundamental differences between the religion of Abraham and Jesus and all the other great religions of the world. These other religions without exception insist that religion is man's search after God. The responsibility lies with the worshipper. What he does; where he goes; how much he gives; what he knows, are all aspects of the process which will lead him to God. In Christianity the traffic is flowing in the opposite direction. It is not so much characterised by man's desire after God, as by God's desire after man.

How clearly I remember my early, confused undergraduate days at Glasgow University. The emotional trauma of my mother's untimely death and the intellectual hurricane of the philosophical thinking which I was forced into as I read Philosophy there, both served to erase most of my preconceived ideas and traditional mind-sets. It happened gradually, but astonishingly swiftly, and I found myself adrift on a sea of doubt. All that I had been led to believe was now seriously under attack and my traditional bulwarks crumbled by the day. I was vulnerable and unable to do anything about it –

apart from feeling the misery of rootlessness. I do not think that I ever doubted the existence of God, but my understanding of God at that time would have been enormously difficult to verbalise. I did seriously question, however, the divinity of Christ, the authority of the Bible, the relevance of the Church and every other belief on which I had been so surely reared. These were difficult years, and I was not easy to live with. In my mental exhaustion and spiritual torpor God came to me gently and unspectacularly. I had no blinding moments of revelation, but I had many arrogant arguments with the eternal God of the universe – He always won. In a number of what, to most, would seem trivial ways, God affirmed the reality of His promises and the validity of His claim that He never promises what He cannot fulfil. Unobtrusively I found myself back on an old shore after a long and chartless night adrift. The shore was the same, but the surroundings were different. They were my surroundings – personal and specific to me. God had done it. I recognised that. He had taken the initiative and come to me 'walking on the water' as I struggled to steer my ship somewhere, I knew not where. I was not always consciously seeking Him through these years, but I know now that, with great longing in His heart, He wanted me – He must have done otherwise He would have cut me adrift for ever on my own endeavours. How I thank God that He takes the persistent initiative and comes to us where we are – in our doubts, confusions, fears, rebellions, obstinacies, sin and shame. God wants to safeguard that basic aspect of His nature – our relationship depends on His willingness and desire to come to us and not the effort we make to find Him. The Son of God became the Son of Man in order that the sons of men might become sons of God.

Thirdly, it replaces God in *attitude*. Speaking of the guilt of mankind in the very first chapter of his letter to the Christians in Rome, the apostle Paul says: 'Instead of worshipping the immortal God, they worship images made to look like mortal man or birds or animals or reptiles . . . They exchange the truth about God for a lie; they worship and serve what God has created instead of the Creator Himself who is to be praised forever'.

So what was no doubt intended to be help becomes hindrance and what was meant to be symbol only becomes substitute for actuality. God will not tolerate any of this. He is jealous for the reality of His own nature and concerned for us that we should embrace fact and not fantasy. God makes it clear that this kind of behaviour is far-reaching and affects not only us, but our great-grandchildren. It continues to be relevant for four generations. Admittedly, there is a very thin dividing line between an image and a religious symbol. The religious symbol is intended to be a reminder of God rather than a representation of God. We need to be careful not to deal with misuse by refusing to use what can be helpful. Proper use is the correct response to misuse. After all, Jesus used material symbols to remind us of spiritual truth. Bread, wine and water all figure in the spiritual heritage God has passed on to us. There are material, visible objects which are helpful in worship and in our appreciation of what God has done for us in Christ. However, we need by faith to go beyond the symbol to touch and experience the reality. Religious symbols need to be carefully regarded for fear they become material images. I was not reared in this tradition, but frequently now we use oil to anoint people for healing. We do this in obedience to the letter of James 5:13–16. Although we have been involved in this for years now it still fills me with great wonder when I realise what I am part of. The oil is not the Holy Spirit, but it represents Him. The value lies not in the amount or quality used, but in the ability of the one being anointed really to receive what is symbolically being applied to his body – the powerful, creative, life-imparting, health-giving Holy Spirit.

Another kind of image of God which we create out of our own experience is a *mental* image. Many times during wars of any kind, and any time, families are split up. During World War II I heard a very credible story of a little boy who was born after his father had returned abroad on active service.

The years passed and the only communication which the husband and father had with his family was by letter. The boy grew up during those years and was told that the man in the large framed photograph over the fireplace was 'daddy'. As he learned to speak, his mother was concerned that he should recognise his father, and so the photograph became quite a feature of the little boy's life. The father was taken prisoner and so his return home was delayed until after the armistice had been signed. It was with great excitement that his return was awaited. The passing of the years, and the effects of the prisoner-of-war camp, significantly changed his appearance. To a little boy's eyes and experience, the man who returned bore little resemblance to the 'daddy' of the photograph. He quite persistently refused to call the reality 'daddy', preferring to relate to the photograph as his father. He had a mental image of what his father was like and that did not allow him to recognise or respond to the reality.

You can build a *material* image of metal or stone or wood or even plastic, but you can also build a *mental* image of whatever substance you choose. The result is that many have a picture of God in their minds which is false. Many of us have a mental image of God which is always in danger of making God in the likeness of our own image. We need to recognise this possibility and realise that God is better, stronger, wiser and much more able than we or any other could ever experience.

Years ago I read Canon J. B. Phillips' book *Your God is too Small* for the first time. I have read it again and referred to it from time to time through these years and have seldom failed to be impressed by Canon Phillips' insights. The chapter headings are worth noting by themselves. Here are some: 'The Grand Old Man' – God is an indulgent, doddery, not very 'with it', over-the-hill grandfather figure. He is not really to be taken seriously by new generations. He is out of touch with things as they are now and anyway He doesn't mind me having a 'bit of fun' from time to time. 'God in a Box' – God is the God of the special occasion and the special place.

Sunday and Church fit Him nicely and He gives a certain something to the grand event. He is certainly not the god of the launderette, the supermarket, the building site, and the busy, noisy, untidy family home. 'Resident Policeman' – His sole purpose is to uphold and enforce the Law. He only really becomes relevant in our experience when we break the Law. He is immediately there to impress upon us our folly, guilt and accountability. 'Perennial Grievance' – He is never satisfied, no matter how well things are going or however well we are doing. He is never appreciative and is always complaining. 'Managing Director' – He is a God who presses all the buttons in some remote upstairs office. When the sound of His button-pressing is heard everyone jumps although they are not always completely certain what they ought to be doing as a result. He is obviously very busy – too busy to be bothered or personally involved in the details of the baby being sick, the car battery being flat, the garden fence having been pushed down, and my anxiety that yet again this month my expenditure is higher than my income. 'Fireman' – God is the God of the crisis. He is neither needed nor wanted in normal circumstances. It is good to know, however, that He is around and can be contacted and will immediately respond with no questions asked initially when the unexpected happens and we push the panic-button. Perhaps the most interesting heading of all is what J. B. Phillips calls 'Assorted' – God is whatever you want and need Him to be in all and every occasion.

The Second Commandment demands that we check what kind of *mental* image we have of God – again for fear that the God we believe in is more fantasy than fact. For most of us our mental picture of God is poles apart from what God has revealed of Himself in creation, through the Bible, and particularly in the founder and finisher of our Faith, Jesus Christ. Jesus did say, 'He who has seen me has seen the Father'. Does our concept match the reality or are we guilty of breaking the Second Commandment with our minds as well as with our hands?

As well as *material* and *mental* images we can also construct *moral* images of God. In the very beginning God said, 'And now we will make human beings; they will be like us and resemble us . . . So God created human beings . . .' So that was the first image of God in history. God created a being like Himself. In the beginning you could look at Adam and say with confidence, 'This is what the invisible God is like!' So quickly that became no longer true, and we are the descendants of that no longer true. How many of us would allow our lives to be scrutinised and investigated in detail, and dare to allow anyone to conclude 'This is what God is really like!'? The image is still there, but it has been blurred, spoiled, stained and badly defaced. For centuries men were without a viable image of the invisible God – so they began to make images.

In the light of all this, what did God do? He made an Adam Mark II. He started a new humanity and began a new race. He said to His own unique Son Jesus, 'You go and be my image on the face of the earth!' Jesus did, and became the visible image of the invisible God. In Him all of God was pleased to dwell. He reflected God's glory without any obstacle and showed God's likeness without any flaw. People again have a '*graven image*' of God! However, this time God has made it, or rather has made Him. To the universal heart-cry expressed through the lips of one of His disciples, Philip, 'Lord, show us the Father; that is all we need', Jesus answered, 'For three years, Philip, you have been looking at God. Why, then, do you say, "Show us the Father"?'

However, we cannot see Jesus *now* – there is no photograph or portrait or sculpture. Jesus has ascended to heaven. His resurrection has taken place and in His glorified body He is in heaven – beyond us! We seem to be back where man was for such a long time. But God has begun to create people like Jesus – and the name of this process is Christianity. Having redeemed men and women His Spirit wants to make them like Jesus. The fruit which the Spirit creates and generates in a human life makes a man or woman like Jesus – so that His *character* is shown once more on the face of the earth. The gifts which the Spirit gives so graciously and undeservedly make the *conduct* of Jesus evident before men once more – so that what Jesus can *do* is displayed alongside what Jesus *is*. This is the cry of the apostle Paul's heart in that classic statement of the implications of the Gospel to the Christians in Rome, 'Those whom God had already chosen He also set apart to become like His Son, so that the Son would be the first among many brothers' (Rom 8:29). Again writing to the confused and careless Christians in Corinth he says, 'Just as we wear the likeness of the man made of earth, so we will wear ("let us wear") the likeness of the man from heaven' (1 Cor 15:9) and 'All of us, then, reflect the glory of the Lord with uncovered faces; and that same glory, coming from the Lord, who is the Spirit, transforms us into His likeness in an ever greater degree of glory' (2 Cor 3:18). And to the Christians at Colosse he writes equally expressively, '. . . you have put off the old self with its habits and have put on the new self. This is the new being which God, its creator, is constantly renewing in His own image, in order to bring you to a full knowledge of Himself' (Col 3:9, 10). The clear message is that God wants visual aids all over the world so that people will know what He is like. But God wants visual aids of His making and choosing, not of ours. You are not to make an image, but you are to let God do it!

The main, powerful thrust of the Second Commandment is that by making images of God – whether material or mental – we are flagrantly dishonouring God because we go on to worship Him and think of Him in an unworthy and inadequate way. Anything which is less than what is revealed in the Bible or in our Lord Jesus Christ is unworthy and unacceptable. However, God's concern is not just because of our attitude towards Him, but also because of the consequences for ourselves. We have already seen that man becomes very like what he worships. The Psalmist openly indicates this reality when he speaks about the one true God in Psalm 115. He describes the mouths, eyes, ears, noses, hands and feet of the idol and how useless these organs are, and then says, 'May all who made them and who trust in them become like the idols they have made'. Perhaps an even better translation would be in the context, and from the actual text, 'All who made them and who trust in them will become like the idols they have made' (v. 8). It is not so much the expression of a desire in his heart as it is a direct consequence of practising idolatry. It is because of this that he says, 'Trust in the Lord . . .' all of you (v. 9–11).

How important it is for us who have now the inestimable privilege of being able to see what God is really like in Christ – for this is God with a robe on, God with sandals on His feet, God eating bread and fish, drinking water and becoming tired. This is God putting Himself into our shoes in order to portray clearly to the human family what He, the Eternal, is really like. How important it is for us not only to look and see and believe, but also to receive what God wants to give us by His Spirit, in order to enable us to become like His Son so that the world will really know that our God reigns and is alive, so that they will become like the one they worship. In this alone lies the hope of the world.

~ 4 ~

Take God seriously

Words need to be taken seriously. God never endorses the flippant, inconsequential phrase 'it's just words'. Words are important and have a profound effect, no matter how they are spoken or when or by whom. 'You can be sure,' Jesus said, 'that on the Judgment Day everyone will have to give account of every useless word he has ever spoken. Your words will be used to judge you – to declare you either innocent or guilty' (Matt 12:36, 37). That was a sobering and solemn declaration, spoken with such simplicity and clarity that no one could ever mistake what was being said.

The Bible says that the human tongue gives direction, for it is like the bit in a horse's mouth which controls whether it moves or stops, turns left or right. It is also like the small, unseen steering mechanism of a great ship – the rudder. The effect is final in the direction which is taken by either. The tongue can also cause destruction. It can be like the spark which starts the forest fire and, as a result, panic-stricken fear and absolute devastation result.

During this century one of the world's best-known and most unforgettable leaders used his tongue with remarkable effect. In 1932 he said with accurate discernment and with nation-shaking passion, 'The streets of our country are in turmoil; the universities are filled with students rebelling and rioting. Communists are seeking to destroy our country, and the nation is in danger – yes danger from within and without. We need law and order! Without law and order our nation cannot survive!' It sounds like the impassioned speech of a party leader at one of the autumn party political conferences, or at least the Home Secretary or Shadow Home Secretary, reacting to yet another terrorist, anarchistic atrocity foisted upon the unsuspecting citizens of our land and brave words are important then. However, these were the words of Adolf Hitler to a country with a collapsing economy and disintegrating stability. In 1930 Germany was in desperate financial straits. Inflation was so severe that thousands were starving. Communism had won the hearts of a significant number and rioting was rife in the streets and pandemonium characterised the universities. The possibility of a complete collapse stared the Republic in the face. Although we may not have lived either within that society, or through those tumultuous times, most of us are now familiar with the rather substandard black and white film archives of some of the speeches delivered to incredible masses of people by Hitler. The analysis was penetrating, the logic convincing, and the passion is still effective after all these years although preserved in a form substandard by modern evaluation. There was something in the voice, the words, the oratory that gave vision and hope, and influenced the desire to meet the challenge of the times with courage and self-sacrifice. Authority was unmistakable in his words. Emotion ebbed and flowed with powerful effect in the cascade of syllables which rehearsed the past glories of the nation, and indignant fury solidly blocked the destructive road of despair that took the nation into its future destiny. The result was ecstatic joy because hope was born and the darkness was glowingly penetrated. The streets rang with the wild response of 'Heil Hitler!' Christians in Germany were persuaded by what he said, and in the 1930s eighty per cent of the evangelical Christians voted for him. His words gave a new direction to a nation. National pride and a positive sense of purpose was re-born. Rioting stopped. Men started working again. The great German autobahns were built. People started eating. Ferdinand Porsche designed the first Volkswagen. Words were being transformed into deeds.

However, as is well known now, Hitler's words brought destruction as well as giving direction—and 35,866,533 civilians and military personnel died in World War II, including 6,000,000 Jews in the awesome phenomenon of the Holocaust. These were the numbers of those who did not survive, but who can record the numbers of those who did and remained and remain physically, socially, mentally, emotionally and spiritually damaged until at last for them, too, death ends the struggle. All of that, the result of a small, complicated organ of skin, muscle, nerve and blood in one man's mouth. The Third Commandment is a salutary reminder to all to watch their tongues. The First Commandment has to do with our *hearts*, the Second Commandment has to do with our *minds* and our *hands*, but the Third Commandment has to do with our *mouths*. God takes words seriously, and we need to take Him seriously.

The world was made by words. In twenty-five verses in the first chapter of the Book of Genesis there is a record that on nine occasions when God spoke, another aspect of creation resulted. Not only was the world made by words, but it is also controlled by words. God intended that the world would be influenced by words. God made man in such a way that he could speak words and so demonstrate his dominion over everything that He had made. As God spoke man obeyed, and as man spoke the world obeyed—that was God's intention. Not only was the world made by words and intended to be dominated by words, but it also fell from God's original intention for it because of words. The devil questioned God's directions and prohibition, and so introduced the first lie and presented the first doubt. The result was chaos and confusion. In the light of this, God's heart and thoughts and love were crystallised in a word—Jesus Christ. In His life and ministry Jesus demonstrated the awesome power of the spoken word. The wind blew with gale force and the waves crashed upon the tiny fishing boats and Jesus said, 'Be still!' and they were. The demons recognised Him as they tormented a man in the Synagogue and Jesus said, 'Be quiet and get out!' and they did. He spoke to a fever and it obeyed Him. He cursed a fig-tree and it shrivelled from its roots upwards. He instructed the nobleman to return home since his son was alive; and the cripple to take up his bed and walk; and the leper to be clean – and it all happened as He said.

No wonder the wise and very practical writer of the Book of Proverbs says, 'You will have to live with the consequences of everything you say. What you say can preserve life or destroy it; so you must accept the consequences of your words' (18:20, 21). No wonder James says so clearly to second-generation Christians, 'All of us often make mistakes. But if a person never makes a mistake in what he says, he is perfect, and is also able to control his whole being. We put a bit into the mouth of a horse to make it obey us, and we are able to make it go where we want. Or think of a ship: big as it is and driven by such strong winds, it can be steered by a very small rudder, and it goes wherever the pilot wants it to go. So it is with the tongue: small as it is, it can boast about great things. Just think how large a forest can be set on fire by a tiny flame! And the tongue is like a fire . . .' (Jas 3:2–6).

The most important implication, however, of the Third Commandment is that it demands that we take God seriously. One of the most amazing – and perhaps one of the most terrifying – events in history occurred nine hundred and eighty-seven years ago. The year was AD 999. Christianity was almost one thousand years old. It was widely believed that Jesus, the Son of God, would return to this planet a thousand years after His first entrance into it. Many were convinced that if He did not return before the millennium was completed, He would certainly return at the first breaking of the dawn of the new millennium. The last decade of the first millennium was characterised by mounting apprehension and anticipation – 990, 991, 992, 993, 994, 995, 996, 997, 998, 999 – and with the birth of the last year before AD 1,000 strange and amazing things began to happen. People began to listen to their Church with a wholehearted seriousness. There was no stealing. Cheating was almost unknown. Bakers gave bread away free of charge. There was a constant cycle of confessions, absolutions, masses and communion. An ancient chronicle describes what is supposed to have taken place on the last day:

> As midnight neared, masters and servants embraced. Offenders forgave each other. There was open repentance and godly sorrow for sin. In the old basilica of St Peter, Pope Sylvester II performed a midnight mass in silence. The church was crowded. Inside, a huge clock ticked once each second. The Pope prayed in silence. The worshippers lay face down, afraid to look up. Suddenly the clock stopped ticking. Hundreds shrieked. Some died of fright. The bell began to strike the midnight hour. Pope Sylvester raised his hands. All the bells rang at once. From the choir loft came the Te Deum Laudamus – to God be glory!

They obviously erred – as many have done since – in their understanding and interpretation of the promise of Christ and the revelation of the Word of God about the return of Jesus to this planet. But they certainly did not err in keeping the spirit and fundamental implication of the Third Commandment. They were taking God seriously, and incidentally left us with an invaluable illustration of what can happen in a world that is prepared to do this too. This is the positive application of this commandment.

Our words certainly and literally declare how seriously we take a situation or a person. Words give a powerful insight into a person's heart – what a person *is* will be seen (and heard) clearly in what he *says*. If you want to know what is in a man's *mind* watch his *mouth*. This is why the Word of God is so important – we know what God is *like* by what He *says*. Over 700 times in the first five books of the Old Testament the writer claims to be giving us the very words of God. In the prophecy of Ezekiel the prophet uses the phrase 'the Lord spoke to me' or its equivalent over 200 times. In the thirty-nine books of the Old Testament it is recorded that God had actually spoken to the writers over 2,000 times. We cannot see God with our physical eyes, touch Him with our physical hands, or hear Him too often with our physical ears – yet He has spoken, and through the generations men have heard Him clearly and responded to what He said. If God were not a God who talked we would not know what He is like. Sometimes we like what we hear, and sometimes we don't. But God is a God who communicates with His people.

Words also have a marked influence on people. The things we say and the way we say them have an effect. In fact, the things we do not say have an effect on people too. I remember travelling one delightful, sunny Sunday evening to preach at a church in the heart of Buckinghamshire. I arrived to find a lady there who showed me to a room where I waited alone until about two minutes before the service was due to begin. A man arrived to let me know that he would take my list of hymns to the organist, and that I should proceed with leading the service in about one minute's time – I did. It was awful. No one seemed particularly interested. When I announced the Scripture lesson no one appeared to have a Bible. The tiny congregation was grouped at the back of the building, so I moved down from the pulpit so that I could be nearer them when I preached. I did preach, but I never completed that sermon – and I don't really think anyone noticed. I closed the service well within the hour – and no one said anything about anything to me. It was a bizarre experience that has left me wondering even after all these years. I think I have been long enough in the ministry not to expect too much, but most of my comments to my family back at home were prefaced with 'I thought they might have said' – but they didn't, and it affected me.

Our words, or lack of them, do affect people and often make it easier for them to do good and harder for them to do wrong, or easier for them to do wrong and harder for them to do good. Our words can certainly stimulate either faith or unbelief. Of course our words can either communicate the greatness of God or they can belittle Him. All of this is enshrined in the Third Commandment, and the negative side of this commandment is a warning against insulting God with our words. When I speak in an empty, meaningless, insignificant, careless and belittling way about God I not only give an insight into my own heart and life, and influence other people in the process, but I also insult the God whom I am talking about in such a way. It is sobering to realise that I cannot speak of God in His absence or behind His back. Whenever I take His name on my lips, I do so to His face.

It would be good to unpack this negative side of the Third Commandment so that we can think our way through to seeing whether we are infringing it or not. The first and most obvious way of infringing this commandment is by profanity. I was brought up to believe that this was all that was meant by it – and the King James version of the Bible certainly encourages that very limited understanding of it. It has a much wider implication than prohibiting the use of bad language involving the name of God. Let it be said, however, that profanity remains prohibited as a consequence of taking the Third Commandment seriously. In a generation which has been brought up on Johnny Speight's Alf Garnett as standard British television humour, with its content directed towards Great Britain, the Queen, the Tory Party and God, it is not unnecessary to underline that God prohibits profanity here. I know that profane people would readily respond and say, 'I'm not really serious, you know!' or 'It's just a habit that I've got into!' or 'It doesn't really mean anything to me' – just so. God does really want us to take Him seriously and to mean something to us. As has happened within our society, profanity has influenced others and God is not taken seriously and means very little to many. As ever our words have an effect on the lives of others. It has not been the only reason, but profanity has made a powerful contribution to a godless society.

There are six other ways, however, in which we infringe the Third Commandment. The King James translation of the commandment is that we are not to 'take the name of the Lord thy God in vain'. In Hebrew the phrase translated 'in vain' literally means 'for unreality'. The word used is the word which the King James version often translates 'vanity'. The word describes that which is empty, idle, insincere, frivolous. In other words we are never to use the name of God in an empty, frivolous or insincere way. This happens in many areas.

1. The area of reassurance

One of the basic problems in human society is to know when someone is telling the truth. We discover, at a very early age, how to tell lies. Parents have to instruct their children on the importance of telling the truth. They never have to instruct their children on how to tell lies – that will happen anyway. Aware of the doubt about whether something is the truth or not, a man will say: 'As God is my judge' or 'God is my witness' or 'God strike me down if I'm telling a lie' or 'God knows I am telling the truth'. In other words a man uses the name of God to bring reassurance that his word can be trusted. How often over the years men and women have come to my door to ask for money. The usual procedure is to tell a long, and often involved, account of their misfortune, and of how some money is necessary for the next couple of days or so to see them through to the end of the month. They have looked into my eyes as I have attempted to respond to their need, and with great sincerity in their voices, have vowed – often using the name of God in some way (after all when they came to the door they were looking for 'the Reverend' and he is into all this about God) – they would repay me. They are attempting to reassure me about the reliability of their story and the sincerity of their promise. In all the years, possibly only two have returned to return what they borrowed. This is how the Third Commandment can be infringed.

Perjury, in law, is to call God to witness and then tell a lie. It is not an inconsiderable thing to do, and when done officially within a law court, and it is discovered, it is a punishable offence. Such is the view of our society of the need to know where the truth lies.

Jesus speaks about oath-taking in his Manifesto of the Kingdom contained in Matthew 5 to 7. He says that it is important in life in the Kingdom of God to say what you mean and to mean what you say. It should be enough for anyone to say simply, 'Yes, I will' or 'No, I won't' (Matt 5:33–37). To have to strengthen your promise with a vow is to show that something is wrong. There is a background to that teaching by Jesus. In the time of Jesus the Jews were masters of evasion. If they did take an oath in the name of God, they kept it, but they would do everything possible to avoid doing so. They would swear by heaven, or by earth, or by Jerusalem, or by their own heads, and they would feel themselves quite free to break such an oath, because it actually did not include the name of God. God, in other words, had not actually been made a partner to the transaction by name, and so the transaction was quite breakable.

Jesus is here (Matt 5:33–37) teaching that heaven is God's throne, and the earth is God's footstool, and Jerusalem is God's city, and so on. The point that He is making is that you cannot possibly keep God out of any transaction, whether His name is used in a technical way or not, for He is everywhere present, and so when a promise is given He is there. All promises and pledges are made in the presence of God and so an oath in the name of God is unnecessary for God is there anyway.

There have been good and honourable people, like the Quakers, who took this as an absolute prohibition and would never take an oath in a law court. But it is clear from the New Testament itself that the prohibition is not as absolute as that, since it must be read against its background of evasion. After all Jesus Himself did not refuse to be put on oath when He was before the High Priest (Matt 26:63). He was asked a question under oath and answered without any comment. Paul gives a solemn pledge using the name of God to the Galatians (Gal 1:20) assuring them that he is telling the whole truth.

It is true that this kind of oath-taking should never be necessary, but clearly there are times when it has to be done.

There are two challenges, however, which the Third Commandment gives. First of all we must always be aware that anything we say and anything we promise is said and promised in the name and presence of God, whether we use the name of God or not. It lays down the sanctity of all promises. A man's word should be his bond whether it is in the day-to-day business of living amongst others, entering into a work contract or a money contract, taking an oath in a court of law to tell the truth, the whole truth and nothing but the truth, vowing to a marriage partner to keep faithful to him/her 'as long as we both shall live', or taking an oath to our Saviour and King Jesus Christ as we eat bread and drink wine in the sacrament of the Lord's Supper. (*Sacramentum* was the Latin word for a vow or pledge of loyalty and allegiance to a commander by a soldier or to an emperor by a citizen.) The other challenge is that an oath is useless where God is not seriously believed in. This is using God's name 'for evil purposes' and is a misuse of His name. In recognition of the godlessness of our society it is now possible to take a simple affirmation in a law court rather than an oath.

It would be wonderful to live in a world where the use of the name of God, or indeed the use of any other device, were unnecessary to give reassurance of the truth. But realistically, the world is the devil's territory and he is the father of lies.

2. The area of ridicule

It is possible to laugh and make fun of the things of God. We need to contest, however, the heresy that laughter is a breach of Christian good manners. The New Testament is a book of joy. It uses the verb 'to rejoice' 72 times and the noun 'joy' 60 times. Someone once asked Rufus Moseley if he thought Jesus ever laughed, to which he replied, 'I don't know, but he sure fixed me up so I can laugh'. Joy certainly is a distinguishing feature of the Christian life and a sign of spiritual maturity. Whatever ingredients are in the Christian life, in whatever proportion, joy has always been one of them. Teaching which leaves a man in dark despair is not Christian. Dr L. P. Jacks has written a little book which he calls 'The Lost Radiance of the Christian Life'.

> Christianity is the most encouraging, the most joyous, the least repressive, the least forbidding of all the religions of mankind. There is no religion which throws off the burden of life so completely, which escapes so swiftly from our moods, which gives so large a scope to the high spirits of the soul, and welcomes to its bosom with so warm an embrace those things of beauty which are joys for ever . . . Christianity does not brood upon the sorrows of mankind. It is always music that you hear, and sometimes dancing as well.

Laughter and humour are positive and creative and can quickly put things in proportion where they are in great danger of getting completely out of focus. We so often take ourselves and others far too seriously. It is good to laugh with others at ourselves – and sometimes with others at them. This need not be cruel or wounding. There is an unwritten assumption that to be spiritual is to be constantly sober and solemn and serious. One of the things which impressed the prosecuting Roman lawyer, Tertullian, causing him to become a Christian and to come down to us from history as one of the early church Fathers, was the obvious joy of the Christians standing trial because of their faith in Jesus Christ, and sometimes in danger of losing their lives as a result. His conclusion as a result of his clinical observation was that 'the Christian saint is hilarious' (latin – *hilaritas*). To him, and to us, the distinction between pleasure and Christian joy was clear. Pleasure depends on our circumstances – either as they affect us or our loved ones, friends or associates, but Christian joy remains when circumstances are not only unkind, but savage, and when every comfort is withdrawn. Pleasure is dependent, not only on the circumstances of life, but it also varies with the changes of life – what brings pleasure to the boy does little for the man. Christian joy is not so dependent.

All of this makes it ludicrous that in the parish records of a Scottish Presbyterian Church there is an entry which says that a couple were fined five shillings for laughing in church. Five shillings was a fortune in those days – and even more so to a Scottish couple! No wonder the atheist James Swinburne looked around on a great deal of the religious scene of his day and concluded:

> Thou hast conquered, O pale Galilean, the world
> has grown grey from Thy breath.

It is a libel on Jesus, however, that He takes all the colour and vitality and joy out of life.

It is possible, nevertheless, to laugh at – in the sense of ridiculing and belittling – the things of God. The Third Commandment challenges that kind of attitude and behaviour. The Bible, for example, never laughs at death. On the contrary it takes it very seriously and regards it as the greatest enemy on earth that man will ever face. To laugh at it could be to help people not to take it too seriously and so make it difficult to assess their eternal destiny. In any case too many people struggle with one of the severe consequences of death – bereavement – to trivialise it and treat it lightly.

Again it is possible to be frivolous over heaven and hell. Both are intensely real and our conversation can quickly and successfully undermine that reality. Never laugh at the furniture of heaven nor the temperature of hell. One is indescribably beautiful, whilst the other is awesomely horrible. To tamper with either is to be in danger of discrediting both.

Satire and ridicule in television humour these days can easily mount a direct onslaught on God Himself. The names by which He is referred to, and the feelings which He undoubtedly has, are not to be the object of empty, idle jesting. God is God and is never to be the object of our irreverent jokes. To ridicule Him in our speech is to create a wrong impression and convey less than reality about Him to those around us—especially to those who do not know His true nature and character from biblical revelation or through a personal relationship in Jesus Christ.

3. The area of reality

Jesus dealt calmly with sins of impulse and passion, but swiftly and heatedly with hypocrisy. In fact the most terrible invective which came from His lips was caused by His discernment and discovery of hypocrisy. His description of some was to call them 'white-washed sepulchres'. They were covering death and darkness with the appearance of life and light. Evil is nasty at any time and sometimes can be quite blatantly nauseous, but when it puts on the cloak of piety and uses the language of religion it becomes a poisonous perversion. Hypocrisy always doubles the sins it covers. This is why God deals with it so severely in the Old Testament (Josh 7) and in the New Testament (Acts 5).

Speech is one of the main ways of presenting hypocrisy—taking words on our lips and in our mouths that are not matched in our lives and in our minds. It is dangerously possible for our mouths to be saying one thing while our minds are thinking another. It is comparatively easy for our lips to be saying one thing whilst our lives are clearly saying another. There must always be a question mark over a person's spiritual credibility on the basis of a profession of faith on its own. In the first two chapters of that intensely personal letter which John, the beloved disciple, wrote in Ephesus, when he was reaching his own centenary, as a loving anxious sermon, he seriously questions the validity of a man's spiritual standing on the basis simply of a profession of faith (i.e. 1:6, 8, 10; 2:6, 9). He is concerned deeply about those who say they love God, but do not show it. Categorically he writes that it is not possible consciously to love God and at the same time blatantly to disobey Him. In this section of his letter John is concerned to identify the true from the false.

Living the good life will always involve saying what we mean and meaning what we say. Using written and set prayers and praying audibly are frequent temptations to hypocrisy. Neither is wrong in itself, but they leave us with the danger of saying to God with our lips what is not in our hearts, simply because that is what we read in the case of set prayers or that is what is expected in the case of audible prayers. Jesus taught a set prayer to His disciples because they asked Him to, but how often it has been misused. At school we used the Lord's Prayer (or better the Disciples' Prayer) every morning at Assembly. But often it was accompanied not with a devoted heart, but with a mental anxiety to learn some French vocabulary or complete a Maths exercise before the actual school day began. We said the right words, but our hearts and minds were occupied and engrossed in other ways. This is not to condemn written and set prayers or audible prayers, but to caution us over one of the ways in which we can become accustomed to hypocrisy of speech.

Hymn-singing is another example of the same thing. Validity of our praise is secured not by the form of worship in which we engage, but by the reality in our hearts which we are expressing. It is possible to sing 'Now thank we all our God, with heart and hands and voices' and to be critical and cynical towards God because of our personal circumstances. It is possible, with raised hands and closed eyes, to sing, 'He is Lord, He is Lord. He is risen from the dead and He is Lord' and yet be intent on having our own way and doing our own thing.

It has become increasingly common to stand in the presence of God and take solemn vows in His name 'to have and to hold from this day forward, for better for worse, for richer for poorer, in sickness and in health, to love and to cherish, until we are separated by death' and to see that as an ideal rather than as a standard. The tide of marital breakdown is rising at a worrying rate, and part of the difficulty is caused by saying one thing and deep down in our hearts recognising that the commitment need not necessarily be either life-long or permanent.

Ted Hegre came from Scandinavian stock and became a businessman in the United States. His religious background was formal rather than real for him. However, the day came when he was personally challenged in a worship service. He listened carefully to the hymns which were being sung and concluded, 'These Christians were singing things which were not real to me'. That did not leave him critical of Christians as it has for many, but rather compelled him to ask why this kind of reality escaped him. It is never enough to say, 'I can't sing that!' It is only enough when we say 'Why can't I?' This led to Ted's recognition of who Jesus was and his response to that. In the years that followed he became one of a small group who committed themselves to follow Christ whatever the cost. So the Bethany Fellowship was born in Minneapolis and became the basis for the development of the largest Christian Publishers in the mid-west of America, and the development of a missionary training programme which has not only trained men and women for missionary service, but has taken responsibility to support them as they scattered at the commission of Christ all over the world. Who can tell the effect of a life which allows unreality of heart to be challenged by reality of word?

4. The area of responsibility

Years ago a lady came to my office. I had had many contacts with her and her husband over a long period. They had enormous difficulties in their marriage. Neither was blameless. On this occasion her body language conveyed a new development. I was hardly prepared, however, for what she was to say to me. 'God has told me,' she said, 'to leave Bill' (not his real name). When I enquired how this had happened, she quickly said that she had been reading her Bible and in the Old Testament (Mic 2:10) she had read, 'Get up and go; there is no safety here any more ...' I didn't know the passage, but the first thing I discovered was that she only received part of the verse, and the second thing was that she had an offer to move in with another man, although, she said, it would not be an immoral relationship. The main issue was that she was making God responsible for conduct in her life that was wrong. Let us be careful that we do not use the name of God 'for evil purposes'. Historically a whole catalogue of crimes has been laid at God's door. God has been made responsible for the Inquisition and the Crusades and many a holy war. Personally there is an increasing freedom to justify behaviour on the grounds that 'God told me' or 'God led me' or even more dangerously 'God wants you to'. God does communicate with His family, but let's challenge the glib spiritualising of our own desires and ambitions. Untold anxiety and confusion has resulted because of an irresponsible and fleshly use of the name of God to enforce and explain human behaviour.

It is not my tradition, but I sincerely respect the tradition which prefaces the preached word with the formula 'In the Name of the Father, and of the Son, and of the Holy Ghost'. However, to make this declaration is to indicate that what is going to be said is really what God believes because He has clearly revealed it. To go on to preach unbiblical doctrine is to be awesomely guilty of conduct which is blasphemous. Blasphemy on television is one thing, but in church it is in quite a different dimension. All the doubters are not in the streets, some are in our pulpits wearing dog-collars.

To claim the name of God for some belief or behaviour which God would not acknowledge is to infringe the Third Commandment.

5. The area of relationships

The work of Jesus on the Cross was not only to bring man into a real relationship with God, but also to bring man into a real relationship with man. In fact the Bible indicates you cannot have one without the other. It insists that you must test the depth and reality of your fellowship with God on the basis of the depth and reality of your fellowship with those around you in His family (1 John 2:9; 3:14, 15; 4:20). Fellowship which is substandard is an inevitable slur on the name of God. Christian fellowship has never been a natural thing – it is not based on temperament, background, environment, age or interest. It is totally supernatural. It is the result of the ministry of God the Holy Spirit. He takes ordinary, different men and women and makes them one – this is the Church. This is why quarrelling and animosity within the Church is not a pity – it is a tragedy. It gives God a bad name.

Never minimise the importance of right relationships in demonstrating and authenticating the one whom we represent. The minister of a church in a tough and difficult parish was criticised because there was an absence of an active evangelistic programme. He was actively and positively engaged in ensuring that the relationships amongst the Christians were honouring God and so becoming stronger and much more significant than they had ever been before. However, he was warned that the church would become inward-looking and die. He replied, 'Yet our concentrating on building up the body and letting the Holy Spirit sort us out has added more to the church in a year than I can remember in many previous years. I believe evangelism will keep flowing only from a healthy body'. One of the powerful agents in evangelism in the early Church was the reality and quality of their relationships. They were not perfect in their fellowship, but it was sufficiently obvious to cause many in a divided and fragmented society to be arrested to ask the question how it became possible.

In Gandhi's autobiography he tells that the core of the message of the gospel of Christ impressed him. In his early days he was in South Africa and he did enquire into Christianity. For several Sundays he attended a church in Pretoria. His earnest enquiring mind, however, concluded, 'The congregation did not strike me as being particularly religious (in touch with God and reality). They were not an assembly of devout souls, but appeared rather to be worldly-minded people going to church for recreation and in conformity to custom'. Gandhi, of course, concluded from that experience among others that there was nothing in Christianity which he did not already better possess.

We give God a bad name, not only by the way we live individually, but also by the way we relate to others within the fellowship of the Church. This is why Jesus urgently and passionately pleads with God on that last night He spent on earth before going to the Cross, 'I pray that they may all be one, Father! May they be in us, just as you are in me and I am in you. May they be one, so that the world will believe that you sent me. I gave them the same glory you gave me, so that they may be one, just as you and I are one: I in them and you in me, so that they may be completely one, *in order that the world may know that you sent me and that you love them as you love me*'. Jesus never doubted that unity would be a powerful authentication of Christianity. Division, apart from immorality and infection, gives God a bad name.

6. The area of revelation

To suggest, declare or give the impression by word, act or attitude that God is less than He has revealed Himself to be is to be guilty of breaking the Third Commandment. What the world needs, and indeed what the Church needs, is to see God as He is. The world will never see it unless and until the Church sees it. Our traditions, our prejudices, our unbelief, our imaginations, our pride have all robbed God of so much of what He really is. So we have presented God to the world in a way that is false—and so misled men.

The whole atmosphere of the age tends to make us minimise what we can expect from God, and yet His word reveals that the extent of legitimate expectation is literally without limits. As though to anticipate our reluctance to ask audaciously, God uses every universal term in our language in His promises to us—whatsoever, whosoever, whensoever, wheresoever, all, any, every.

Long ago when a bewildered and reluctant Moses

apprehensively protested his uncertainty about who he would tell others had sent him, he received a reply from God which has reverberated down the centuries (Exod 3:13). The name that God gave Moses in His reply is not so much a name as a description, 'Tell them that *Yahweh* sent you!' The English transliteration of the Hebrew word is *Jehovah*. It literally comes from the verb 'to be' and is accurately translated 'I am'. There were many gods around at that time. For example, in Egypt there were gods like Amon, which meant 'hidden' or 'concealed'. It changes the whole face of prayer to address God as 'Dear hidden/concealed . . .' Another god was Rah, which meant 'swift'. Again to address God as 'Dear swift . . .' makes a living and realistic relationship difficult! What does *Yahweh* tell us about God? It reminds me that God is *personal* – for He is 'I' am. This personal pronoun is intensely personal and must always serve to remind us that God is not a force or a concept or an element. *Yahweh* is a constant reminder also that God is *eternal* – He is I am, not I was or I will be. He never changes from being eternally present. It is a reminder, too, that God is *unique*, for you cannot describe Him in any other way than by saying He is what He is. You cannot compare Him to anyone or anything else. If that were not enough, *Yahweh* clearly indicates that God's name is *incomplete*. In normal language 'I am' is usually followed by something else. Four lines probably indicate this more clearly than any other expression of this aspect of God's character:

When God would teach mankind His Name,
  He calls Himself the Great I Am
And leaves a blank – believers may
  Supply those things for which they pray.

So to the believer who becomes aware of his weakness and desperate inadequacy and so his need for strength, God says, 'I am strength'. To the believer who is overwhelmed by wrong and unacceptable attitudes and feelings and so his need for supernatural love, God says 'I am love'. The Hebrews very quickly learned the wonderful implication of this revelation of God and they did just that, for they took *Yahweh* and put Hebrew words after it. This has come down to us centuries later with all its thrilling relevance. God is Jehovah-jireh – the Lord will provide (Gen 22:13, 14); Jehovah-rophi – the Lord who heals (Exod 15:26); Jehovah-nissi – the Lord is my banner who puts the enemy to flight (Exod 17:8–15); Jehovah-shalom – the Lord is our peace (John 6:24); Jehovah-tsidkenu – the Lord is our righteousness (Jer 23:6); Jehovah-roi – the Lord is my shepherd (Ps 23:1) and so on. Strange as these words may sound in modern Western ears, never was there a greater need or a more bewildered culture to receive them.

The Third Commandment is one of the commandments which will never be seriously regarded as having gone out of date. It is the yearning heart-cry of God to take Him seriously. 'Listen to me!' He cries. 'Take me and my word and my work seriously. I cannot give you peace, or praise, or power, if you will not take my word, my will and my way seriously and sincerely.' The good life will forever escape us unless and until we stop playing with God and take Him seriously.

5

Like Father, like Son

When God made man, He made him like Himself. Unhappily we have reversed the process in our contemporary culture – and we have made God in our image. Therein lies the source of many of our problems. However, the clear reason for responding to the direction of this Fourth Commandment is that this is how God behaves, and so we should do so too. Like Father, like son!

Most of us have an attitude towards Sunday which is directly inherited from our upbringing or is in reaction to it. Nowhere is tradition more rampant and more formative than in our understanding of, and our response to, the Fourth Commandment. The result is that it is difficult to come to this teaching with an open mind prepared to absorb biblical revelation. Some toes will be sore as a result of reading this chapter – because they have been trodden on. Nevertheless, our concern is to investigate with integrity what the Bible actually does say, and then attempt to translate the principle into practice.

My own memories of Sunday are vivid. It began later than any other day in our home. We were a Christian family, and Sunday morning service was the focal point of the morning, but it did not begin until 11.30 a.m. This timing had been agreed on many years previously when life on a Saturday had been pretty hectic and for many it was a working day, with the shops open late into a Saturday evening. The following day was the only one in the week for a late 'lie-in'. The fact that by the time of my boyhood years things were changing made no difference to the late beginning of a Sunday – nor has it in the church of my childhood to this day.

Our town was a pleasant mid-Scotland, semi-industrial town, with a population around 50,000. It was like many other towns in the Forth-Clyde Valley, and on Sunday it was significantly quiet, and, so far as the streets were concerned, empty. Traffic and people seemed to have withdrawn to their respective resting places for the day. Admittedly, car ownership was not the norm in our town, and public transport was severely restricted on a Sunday.

The influence of Scottish Presbyterianism still prevailed, and at the appointed hour of 11.30 a.m. many were found in church. Most walked there, and I recall that the streets in the twenty-five minutes prior to the beginning of public worship were busy with Sunday-dressed men, women and children making their unimpeded way to their various churches, hurrying for fear of being late. The routine of breakfast, getting dressed, and the time it took to get from home to church had all been worked out long years before, and the same people met at exactly the same spot week by week – rain, hail or shine. To the second, the church bells began to ring and stopped ringing – no need for Big Ben or bleeping digital watches in those days. When the 'wee bell' began its insistent unmelodious striking, that indicated that time was short then before the beginning of the services, and the pace noticeably quickened in those who had unhappily been delayed and in those who were always late anyway. It was all so predictable, so comfortable, so secure – so us.

Approximately an hour later the quiet streets were filled with people again, going in the opposite direction with their gastric juices already flowing freely with little chance of being satisfied for some time to come since the oven-timer was a rarity and the microwave oven had not yet seen the light of day. The rest of the day was 'dead' – there were no open shops, little traffic and even less movement. A summer Sunday afternoon saw a number out walking, children making their unhurried and, one sensed, often unwilling, way to Sunday School, and that was all. Evening services were held, but appeared to have little appeal, and the outbreak of the Second World War and the 'black-out' restrictions further decreased their viability. Who said they were necessary anyway, since they had begun more as a result of social pressure and the advent of gaslight than because of pressing spiritual necessity? To be a 'twicer' (as our minister used to say) may have fed spiritual vanity, but it seemed to do little to increase spiritual maturity. The time for meeting together, and the purpose of meeting together, always need to be kept under serious review for fear that we adopt a routine and structure and miss the reason for it.

I recall Sunday in our own home with some pleasure. Although it was busy and the routine was fairly rigid, yet there were a number of compensations. For example, it was the only day that we were all together as a family. The eating arrangements were very satisfactory as far as I was concerned, since a cooked breakfast was followed by a magnificent three-course lunch (prepared always on the Saturday!) and a Scottish high tea that remains a mouth-watering memory to this day because of my mother's baking expertise. A long-lie was followed by morning church, afternoon Sunday School and evening service – and all on the hoof since neither public nor private transport was available or affordable (and I have a sneaking suspicion, even to this day, would not have been thought acceptable).

Sunday clothes were in vogue and I, and all the others in my family, had special Sunday clothes from the skin out and from head to foot. These were removed after morning church, after Sunday School, and finally after evening service before we finally dropped into bed having had a very busy day.

As a child, play on a Sunday was disallowed both inside and outside our home – not that there was much time for it anyway! We often had guests to Sunday dinner, who sometimes were still with us at Sunday tea – and by and large I enjoyed that. Occasionally we would gather round the piano to sing hymns – and that was tolerable too. My father always practised 'his hymns' before going out to Sunday School where he was the Superintendent for about thirty years. He didn't play well, but he sang lustily and so his mistakes were rarely noticed.

Such was my Sunday. I accepted it – and I suppose I will never know whether my acceptance was because I was too docile and lacking in spirit to do anything in the way of protesting or simply that I appreciated Sunday as I found it. It was predictable and secure in years fraught with great uncertainty both domestically and nationally. The impact upon me, however, was much more profound than I realised and there remained a deep, subconscious conclusion that this was the way that God wanted His day to be observed – both in spirit and in detail. It was to take years before I was prepared to think through the way Sunday was to be spent in the light of Scripture, and, where changes in attitude and activity occurred, not to feel guilty that this was less than the best.

I have come now to a firm conclusion that not only do Christians in different parts of the world have profound differences in the way they use their Sunday, but even in this country there is a wide spectrum of practice based on firm biblical principle. Many have thought this through carefully and come to honourable and honest conclusions. It is important to honour the integrity of those whose practice is different from ours. The way that we will follow here is to look first of all at the pattern of Scripture, and then to look at the practice of the early Church in as far as we can locate it, and then attempt to draw some guidelines for ourselves today. Recent legislation and social concern have raised this issue for both Christian and non-Christian alike, and it is important that our convictions are based on truth rather than on tradition. The last time that the House of Commons debated the Sunday Laws a group of responsible, Bible-believing ministers and laymen met to produce a book which would give specific guidance to modern Christians. The book was never written since they could not find agreement among themselves, far less lay down guidelines for others. Perhaps there is an inevitability about this since the Ten Commandments were addressed to the individual within society and not to society in general. 'You' at the beginning of each Commandment is in the singular and these Commandments are concerned with personal behaviour.

This Fourth Commandment, as it stands within the Ten Commandments, is primarily a great piece of social and humanitarian legislation. In the first instance it is not really a religious regulation at all. There is nothing said about the content of worship or about the nature of religious services. What is laid down is a day of rest on which even the serving men and women lay aside their tasks and on which even the toiling beasts are not forgotten. The stranger and the foreigner are to be included in this behaviour. In its original form the Fourth Commandment is supremely one of the great merciful laws of the Old Testament. It is social legislation based on religious belief. Like all of God's directions it is neglected and disregarded at our peril. An old Greek proverb said that the bow which is always bent (i.e. always stretched taut) will soon cease to shoot straight. Historically this is proven. In the days of the French Revolution, the revolutionaries abolished everything that had to do with religion. They abolished Sunday, only to find that they had to bring it back again because the health of the nation was suffering because there was no day of rest. It is a known fact, confirmed by those who study the technique of work, that, if a worker is working really hard, his efficiency diminishes towards the end of the week and his efficiency is restored by a day of rest. Today the 'Friday car' is proverbial and stretches beyond the confines of the motor trade. It has been proved that a day of rest is a social and industrial necessity without which health and work inevitably suffer.

It is here, however, that we run into difficulty with the Fourth Commandment. There is little difficulty in getting agreement with the general principle; the difficulty lies in the practical application of it. In the Old Testament the position of the Jew was quite clear. The Sabbath was one thing which distinguished him from other races and people. The other two things which completed his distinctiveness among others were that he was circumcised and he ate kosher food. The Sabbath clearly was to be a day of rest. No work was to be undertaken on that day. It was to be a day which was to be kept holy. The root definition of the word holy is *different*. The difference of this day was to be demonstrated in that no work was to be done. The reason given for refraining from work is that God doesn't work a seven-day week. When God made man He made him like Himself, and this is how God behaved. We are to behave in the same way as God did. This distinguishes man from every part of nature, for no other part of nature has a Sabbath rest. Saturday, Sunday and Monday are all the same in the plant and animal world.

The extent of the Jewish devotion to the Sabbath Law can best be seen from the fact that at the beginning of the Maccabean struggles the Jews would stand and be killed in cold blood without defending themselves rather than take up arms on the Sabbath day (1 Macc 2:29–38). In the later struggles against Pompey they would stand and watch their enemies building a vast mound from which to attack the city, and deliberately doing the work on the Sabbath, and they would not lift a finger to stop them lest they should break the Sabbath Law (Josephus, *Antiquities of the Jews*, 14.4.2). The Sabbath Law was dearer than life itself. From the beginning, the Sabbath Law was taken seriously and was certainly not regarded as an optional extra.

If the issue is work – and that seems to have been the case – then how are we to define work? It was to answer this question that the scribes began to write down other rules. Originally this was perfectly straightforward and sincere, although the results were to border on the bizarre. Thirty-nine classifications were laid down called 'fathers of work', each classification capable of infinite subdivision. One class of work which was forbidden, for example, was carrying a burden. But what is a burden? Can a man lift his child on the

Sabbath? Yes, he may, but not if the child has a stone in his hand, for the stone is a burden even if the child is not. A burden was defined as

> Food equal in weight to a dried fig; enough wine for mixing in a goblet; milk enough for one swallow; honey enough to put upon a wound; oil enough to anoint a small member; water enough to moisten an eye-salve; paper enough to write a customs-house notice upon; parchment enough to write, 'Hear, O Israel'; ink enough to write two letters of the alphabet; reed enough to make one pen.

And so on and on. In the Mishnah (a summary of the oral law) the section on the Sabbath has 24 chapters. In the Jerusalem Talmud (a commentary and explanation of the Mishnah) the Sabbath section has 64½ columns. In the Babylonian Talmud the Sabbath section extended to 156 double-folio pages. It was forbidden to tie a knot, to light a fire, to move a lamp, to go on a journey, to prepare a meal on the Sabbath. It was forbidden to heal on the Sabbath. In the case of illness or injury, steps could be taken to keep a man from getting worse, but not to cure him or make him better. The scribes carefully worked out these rules and regulations and the Pharisees carefully kept them. So the whole character of the Sabbath was affected. Instead of being a day designed to protect the rights and health and spiritual welfare of man, it became a day of prohibitions, with a list of things which might not be done stretching out into an almost endless series of rules and regulations. It was with this list that Jesus collided and inevitably trouble resulted.

Centuries of subjugation to greater nations robbed the Jews of all possibilities of outward expansion and drove the nation in upon itself. Their scholars and theologians began to study their own laws with microscopic precision. So the original principles were expanded into rules and regulations which covered every conceivable event which might happen to anyone. The need for definition became an obsession, and what was intended by God to be a blessing was made a burden by man. It seems ludicrous to us today – and presumably was every bit as farcical then – that looking in a mirror was discouraged lest the person who was doing the looking saw a grey hair and plucked it out. This was to be regarded as harvesting. Harvesting is work and work is forbidden on the Sabbath day. They did not laugh because they were fully persuaded that they were honouring God. We need to be careful about some of the traditions which we have built into our own attitudes and activities on a Sunday, lest they are every bit as absurd and equally of as little consequence to God.

What God had intended for man's good had deteriorated into something laughable and unhelpful by the time of Jesus. Instead of a day which was intended to lift and inspire man, a day had developed which depressed and burdened him. This largely was the situation which had developed in the Old Testament, and underlay all the record of God's dealings with man there, in all its thrilling revelation of mercy and righteousness. Perhaps one of the main helpful consequences of this legalistic Jewish approach to the Laws of God was that they affirmed that the Sabbath began at sundown on the Friday evening and continued until sundown on the Saturday. In hotel lobbies, and other public places, today signs are to be seen which say something like: 'The Sabbath begins today at 6.16 p.m.' That was the official time of sundown on the Friday evening. On the next day the sign was changed to read: 'The Sabbath ends today at 6.16 p.m.' The Sabbath does not begin at 10.00 in the morning and finish right after dinner – it was and is a 24-hour day. It would be such a good thing for Christians to embrace this and allow Sunday to begin on the Saturday night. How often Sunday morning worship has been a travesty of reality simply because of the way we have spent Saturday evening. The big match and the late film have often been the culprits.

Get up, get up for Jesus, ye soldiers of the Cross,
For Sunday morning spent in bed is sure and certain loss.
If Christians on a weekday can be at work by seven,
Then surely on a Sunday they can worship at eleven.

It was into this situation that the Son of God was born. As a Jew He kept the Law – every bit of it! Clearly for Him the Sabbath was certainly to be used for fellowship with God's people and worship (Luke 4:16). Yet He was unwilling to endorse the rules and regulations which men had imposed on the Sabbath. The Laws of God were one thing, but the inflexible interpretations of men were another. I think Jesus would have enormous difficulty with some of our Church Constitutions and the rigid and uncompromising ways in which we apply these rules – sometimes elevating them to the level on which we would regard Scripture itself. As it would today, so then it caused the greatest conflict with the religious authorities. So fiercely were they prepared to defend their interpretation of the Sabbath Law that they were even prepared to plot the death of God incarnate when it seemed to them that He was infringing what they had decided (e.g. Mark 2 and 3). Jesus not only disregarded the rules and regulations of men Himself, but when it appeared to the religious authorities that His disciples had broken them, He defended them in simple, direct words. On one occasion 'some Pharisees and teachers of the Law came from Jerusalem to Jesus and asked him, "Why is it that your disciples disobey the teaching handed down by our ancestors? They don't wash their hands in the proper way before they eat!" Jesus answered, "And why do you disobey God's command and follow your own teaching?"' There is a powerful caution here because the world has often been put off, not so much by God and His word, as by man and his traditions. The attitude that we adopt and the way we go about fulfilling God's Law has often been the stumbling-block for others rather than God's Law itself.

Jesus clearly saw the Sabbath in a very positive way. It was a day not simply for putting your feet up, but a day for restful, restorative activity. The Jews said, 'It is a day to *stop* doing things', but Jesus said, 'It is a day for *doing* things'. It is not a *negative* day, but a very *positive* one. Fundamentally it is a day to rest from your own work in order that you can give attention to the work of God. When it says in Genesis 2,

> And so the whole universe was completed. By the Sabbath day God finished what He had been doing and stopped working. He blessed the seventh day and set it apart as a special day, because by that day He had completed His creation and stopped working,

the question needs to be asked: 'What did God do on the seventh day when He rested?' It is important for us to think about this if we are going to have a right attitude and response to the Fourth Commandment. In a real sense the seventh day is still continuing today. God was at work in creation for six days – not necessarily six days of twenty-four hours duration, for Scripture does not require such an exclusive interpretation to affirm that creation was directly in the hands of God. There were the six days of God, and the seventh day has lasted a long time too! God is still in His seventh day! What is He doing now? He is working for man's good. This is precisely how Jesus justifies the miracle of healing which He performed on the Sabbath. 'My Father', He said, 'is always working, and I too must work' (John 5:17). The Greek verb which is used here – *ergazomai* – means to 'labour' 'minister' 'trade'. This is how Jesus speaks of God's activity on the Sabbath. In other words God has been involved in the specific work of creation for six days, but He has not ceased His activity. He has stopped doing His own work and now is engaged in working for man's good.

In the same way for man the Sabbath is a time for stopping our own work and starting doing something for God – and so probably for someone else. Jesus made it clear that the Sabbath was for doing good – not indulging yourself. In the third chapter of the Gospel of Mark there are a number of verdicts on Jesus given – those who were diseased saw Him as a miracle-worker (v.7–10); the demons saw Him as the Messiah (v.11); the disciples acknowledged Him as the Master (v.13–18) with authority to call and commission them; His family concluded He was mad (v.20–30); and the crowd could see no further than the fact that He was a man (v.31–35). But the chapter begins in an atmosphere of suspicion and condemnation. People were present in the synagogue for the wrong reason – they wanted 'to accuse Jesus of doing wrong; so they watched Him closely to see whether He would cure the man on the Sabbath'. Jesus was aware of this hostile climate so 'He asked the people, "What does our law allow us to do on the Sabbath? To help or to harm? To save a man's life or destroy it?"' Often our taboos and scruples have blinded us to the real, positive possibilities of the day. Jesus did not teach Sabbath observance in a negative sense – it was not to be a day for not doing things. It was to be a day for doing things. It is this challenge that He leaves us by His behaviour and response to those who would have it otherwise. By implication He is clearly saying: 'You Jews have made man the means and the Sabbath the end, whereas the intention of God is that the Sabbath is the means and man is the end.' In that well-remembered incident where He is walking with the disciples through some wheat fields on the Sabbath and He is criticised for allowing His disciples to pick heads of wheat, He concludes, 'The Sabbath was made for the good of man; man was not made for the Sabbath' (Mark 2:27). The Sabbath is important, but get it into perspective and see that it is there for man's good; to serve man and enrich and encourage him; to help him and not to hinder him. He ends His rebuke to those who condemn Him for the way that He behaves, and allows others to behave, with a categorical statement 'the Son of Man is Lord even of the Sabbath' (Mark 2:28). In other words, 'I am in charge of the Sabbath'; 'I decide what goes on on the Sabbath'.

Significantly, Jesus did not demonstrate His defeat of death on the Sabbath – He rose from the grave on a normal working day. Pentecost did not occur on the Sabbath so initiating the new body of Christ on earth – the Church. God poured out His Spirit in that remarkable Pentecostal effusion on a normal working day. Had these two events occurred on the Jewish Sabbath it would have confirmed Sabbath observance forever, and we would have been meeting for worship and fellowship together on a Saturday rather than on a Sunday. This would have been to invest the Sabbath with a far deeper meaning than ever before. In view of the strategic and fundamental importance of the resurrection of Jesus, it does seem that Jesus was making a clear and definite break. After all it was God who raised Him from the dead to authenticate His life and ministry and person. And so there is a tension for us in the life and attitude of Jesus towards the Sabbath. On the one hand He clearly endorsed it, and on the other He changed it to the point of elimination.

With response to Christ two things happened. All the first Christians were Jews and in the beginning they would naturally worship as their fathers had done, even if they put a new meaning and content into worship. It would not occur to these early Christians that the Sabbath was anything less than binding on them too. However, there was another day which was bound to be a supremely sacred day to them – the first day of the week, because it was on that day that their Lord and Saviour had risen from the dead (Matt 28:1; Mark 16:2; Luke 24:1; John 20:1). They might still observe their ancestral Sabbath, but for them the first day of the week was the day on which the supreme event of history had occurred – the Resurrection.

There are clear signs in the New Testament itself that the first day of the week, the day of the Resurrection, is becoming the Christian day. The Sabbath is not listed as one of the essentials which Gentile Christians must recognise and observe following the strategic Council of Jerusalem (Acts 15:20, 29). It was on the Saturday evening (i.e. after the Sabbath was officially over) that Paul paid his last visit to Troas and they shared fellowship and ministry (Acts 20:7). In a practical way the Christians at Corinth are instructed to put something aside for the collection for the Jerusalem Church 'every Sunday' (1 Cor 16:2). They are falling in line with Paul's instructions elsewhere. The expression 'the Lord's Day' occurs for the first time in Revelation 1:10. It is not the Day of the Lord – as some have inferred with its strong eschatological implications – but the Lord's Day. The two phrases the 'Day of the Lord' and the 'Lord's Day' are two quite different phrases in Greek, and they are never interchangeable. No, quite clearly, we have the first instance of the Lord's Day to describe the first day of the week, the day of the Resurrection, the great day of the Christian Church.

The Jewish Sabbath tended to become increasingly a day of restrictions and regulations and rules and prohibitions. The spirit in which these were taught and observed was harsh and legalistic. Paul, who was the apostle to the Gentiles and very precise, careful and clear about what he taught under the guidance of the Holy Spirit, never once tells these early Christians to observe a weekly day of rest. In fact, quite positively, he instructs them not to observe the Sabbath (Rom 14:5, 6; Gal 4:8–11; Col 2:16, 17). There was a strong move away from the harsh legalism of the Sabbath to the resurrection joy of the first day of the week.

In theory it was possible to observe both the Sabbath and the first day of the week – since the former commemorated creation whilst the latter was a remembrance of the Resurrection. However, it is clear that it was not practical to have two holy days in one week. All Christians in the early Church did two things on a Sunday – they worshipped and they worked. This went on for the first 300 years of Christianity. Jewish Christians worked on a Sunday because it was a normal working day – and if there was a weekly holiday it was the Sabbath for them! Gentile Christians worked on Sunday since there was no such thing as a weekly rest day in the Roman Empire – they had two or three days holiday per month. For the first 300 years of the Christian Church services were held early in the morning and late at night on

Sunday so that work could continue within society.

A series of factors caused the Lord's Day to become a day when no work was to be done. Heathen festivals were in vogue; the strong influence of the Jewish Sabbath; and the fact that Christianity had begun to influence the higher ranks of society where people could, if they so desired, observe a workless Lord's Day; and as the Church became increasingly more organised a greater stress was laid on the obligatory nature of the services of the Church. All of these factors influenced the Lord's Day to become a specifically religious day.

In AD 321, however, the Roman Emperor, Constantine, passed an Act which had significant effect so far as the Lord's Day was concerned. It stated that work must stop in the cities on the Lord's Day, though farming was allowed to continue in the rural areas for fear that crops would be spoiled through inactivity. Eusebius, who has contributed with insight and accuracy to Church history, says that Constantine ordained that one day should be a day of prayer because he was concerned, 'gradually to lead all mankind to the worship of God'. Theodosius (AD 386); the Council of Orleans (AD 538); and the Council of Macon (AD 585) all extended, gave content to, and firmed up the observance of the Lord's Day within society. However, it was Alcuin (AD 735–804) who first identified the Sabbath and the Lord's Day – and all work on the Lord's Day became a breach of the Fourth Commandment. This was a reversal of the practice and conviction of the early Church. Thomas Aquinas (AD 1225–1274) did exactly the same thing, and the identification of Sabbath and Lord's Day was now a fact of life.

With the coming of the Reformation there was unanimity among the Reformers that the Sabbath and the Lord's Day were not the same. Luther, in the Larger Catechism, insists that serving men and maids must have a day of rest and refreshment when they can gather to hear God's Word, and to praise and to pray. But, in principle, it did not matter which day it was. It was not necessarily a fixed day as it was for the

Jews, for in itself one day is no better than another. John Calvin adopted the same position by declaring 'it being expedient to overthrow superstition, the Jewish holy day was abolished, and as a thing necessary to retain decency, order and peace in the church another day was appointed for that purpose'. Again, he said, 'the observance of days among us is a free service and void of all superstition'. The Reformers' position is summarised in the Helvetic Confession: 'The Lord's Day itself ever since the apostles' time was consecrated to religious exercise and to a holy rest . . . Yet herein we give no place to the Jewish observance of the day or to any superstitions. For we do not count one day to be holier than another, nor think that mere rest itself is acceptable to God. Besides, we do celebrate and keep the Lord's Day, and not the Jewish Sabbath, and that with a free observance.' 'There can be no doubt,' said Calvin, 'that, on the advent of our Lord Jesus Christ, the ceremonial part of the commandment was abolished.'

However, the confusion caused by the identification of the Sabbath and the Lord's Day remained. When the Puritans came to power an even more severe series of Sunday Observance Laws was passed (1644 and 1656). One of these laws forbade 'all vain and profane walking' on the Sabbath. So the Lord's Day had become the Jewish Sabbath, and Sabbatarianism was established. Nowhere was this identification of the Sabbath with the Lord's Day more powerful in its effect than in my own native Scotland. Maurice Lindsay in his *Portrait of Glasgow* says that on the so-called Sabbath day 'some people did not sweep or dust the house, nor make the beds, nor allow any food to be cooked or dressed' while others 'opened only as much of the shutters of their windows as would serve the inmates to move up and down, or an individual to sit at the opening to read'. He tells how the first Sunday train ran from Glasgow to Edinburgh on the 13th March, 1842. A journalist wrote at the time that it was 'filled with peaceful and respectable persons, gliding quietly away on its mission'. The Presbytery of the Church of Scotland in

Glasgow denounced the running of trains on Sunday as

> a flagrant violation of the law of God as expressed in the Fourth Commandment, a grievous outrage on the religious feelings of the people of Scotland, a powerful temptation to the careless and indifferent to abandon the public ordinances of Grace, and most disastrous to the quiet of the rural parishes along the line of the railways, by the introduction into them every Sabbath of many of the profligate and dissipated who inhabit the cities of Glasgow and Edinburgh.

In the same book, Maurice Lindsay records: 'In Edinburgh a threatening battery of ministers . . . lined the platforms and informed the detraining passengers that they had bought tickets to hell, a claim which does not seem to have deterred many of them from making their way towards Princes Street.' The extremity of Sabbatarianism was reached when 'an Irish family destitute on the street on a snowy January night in 1847 with one child out of seven dead, the mother herself dying of consumption' were 'victims of a church ruling that soup kitchens for the destitute were not to be opened on the Sabbath for fear of offending the Lord'. Much further than this it is not possible to go!

It is true that historically the pendulum has swung one way and then the other and confusion has resulted. However, in history the principle at issue has been whether the Sabbath and the Lord's Day can be brought practically together and one become identified with the other. Neither the early Church nor the Reformers identified the former with the latter, and the identification of the Sabbath with the Lord's Day did not emerge until the eighth century. Contested by the Reformation this identification of the one with the other emerged again in an even stronger way in the sixteenth and seventeenth centuries. This identification has really been the prime cause of the confusion which has resulted. They are different days commemorating different events – the Sabbath is the last day of the week and commemorates God's rest after the toil of the week of creation, and the Lord's Day is the first day of the week commemorating the Resurrection life and hope of our Lord Jesus Christ.

The Sabbath is the shadow preceding the reality, and when you have the reality, the shadow is not so important any more – substance is more important than shadow. The reality is the Sabbath rest of God. The writer to the Hebrews speaks of it in his letter (4:1–13). He teaches that the Sabbath is not really a day at all, but the rest that comes into your soul when you stop trying to be good enough to earn God's favour and secure your place in heaven. This is the Sabbath rest which belongs to the people of God – 'We who believe, then, do receive that rest which God promised' (4:3). God wants all of us to enjoy and experience this all the time every day of the week. We are to cease from our works and let Him do His work within us and through us. This is what the Sabbath was meant to foreshadow. Our salvation begins, not with a big *do*, but with a big *done*. We have the reality as Christians in Christ, so why should we still want the shadow? If you are really *trusting* in the completed, perfect work of God in Christ for us, and for all, why should we go back to *trying*? We are resting from our own works and efforts to win and earn God's favour and enjoying God's peace in our hearts. Why go back to rules and regulations about days? This is hard teaching for us to receive for two reasons. First of all, there is a strong Sabbath-keeping tradition which is in the past of many of us. Secondly, there is something strongly present within our human nature which wants to earn God's favour and be good enough to deserve it. But grace and merit are opposites and mutually exclusive.

The Sabbath is the Jewish shadow indicating something real to come, because a shadow requires substance to make it a shadow. But Sunday is the glorious celebration of our rest in Jesus.

It's not by works of righteousness
  But by His grace alone
That we are complete in Him.

There's nothing more that I can do
  For Jesus did it all
And we are complete in Him.

The real question is not 'how shall we observe the Sabbath?', but 'how shall we keep Sunday?' and so remember that Jesus is alive because He has risen from the dead and left the tomb empty, and therefore He is with us here and now. We can answer the question by submitting to legalism – that is, we can draw up a list of rules and regulations affirming things you must or must not do. This then becomes a negative thing of imposed duty. The positive side of legalism is to affirm, however, that 'You have six days in which to do your work'. If we are concerned to be legalistic one workless day involves six working days.

Secondly, you can surrender to licence. This is the opposite of legalism. You can say, 'I will do what I like with Sunday', 'I will go where I want on Sunday', 'If I want to do something, I will do it!' Licence, however, is not to be confused with freedom. Sunday is not best kept by doing what I like. Invariably this leads to a boring Sunday for many – with jammed roads in the summer and television and newspaper saturation in the winter.

Thirdly, you can affirm your liberty. You can consciously and positively affirm that Jesus is Lord of every day including Sunday. You can, by an act of your will, look into the face of your heavenly Father and affirm 'your command is my wish', 'I only want to do on a Sunday what you would really like me to do – what you desire, I desire'. Let Him decide what is to be done. In this sense, liberty is much more difficult than legalism. Rules and regulations are already determined and so I need no longer be sensitive to the gracious, gentle unpredictability of the loving, Father heart of God – He knows our need, and with infinite variety wants to meet it. On Sunday I am free from my own works, not so that I would put my feet up, but so that I can be free to do His works. I am free to worship, to enjoy fellowship, to spend it differently from other days, and to use it specially for God. There is no train to catch; shop to open; deadline to meet; letters to dictate; employer to satisfy; employees to reason and negotiate with. It is intended to be the greatest day of the week; the most exciting day; an oasis in the desert; an inspiration affecting the whole of life.

A young man who is now a vital part of our church, and who had lived a pretty dissolute life in a sophisticated way resulting in a broken marriage and a number of very sad and bewildered lives, said to me some time ago, 'From being the most boring day of the week, it has become the most exciting'. And it is! I preached one Sunday morning in Manila in the Philippines, and afterwards a man, a Philippino lawyer who had been baptised only the previous Sunday, spoke to me and said, 'Sunday used to be my day for drinking and it left me depressed with life and despairing about my future, but now it is a day of hope that refreshes and recharges me for the week ahead'.

The way the early Church used Sunday makes instructive reading. The first description doesn't come from a Christian at all, but from Pliny, the governor of Bythinia, to Trajan, the Roman Emperor, in AD 111. Pliny relied on Trajan's help to deal with problems that arose. One of those problems was what to do with Christians – should he treat them as law-breakers, evil-doers and criminals? So he examined and investigated the Christians before he wrote to Trajan. He said:

> They were in the habit of meeting on a certain fixed day before it was light, when they sang in alternate verses a hymn to Christ as to a god, and bound themselves by a solemn oath not to commit any wicked deeds, but never to commit any fraud, theft or adultery, nor deny a trust, when

they should be called upon to deliver it up, after which it was their custom to separate, and then to reassemble to partake of food – but food of an ordinary and innocent kind.

Although this letter shows little insight and understanding, this must have been how it appeared to an onlooker. Coming from a Roman governor it makes its own appeal.

The second description comes from Justin Martyr (c. AD 150) writing to the Roman government in defence of Christianity:

On the day called Sunday all who live in cities or in the country gather together in one place, and the memoirs of the apostles or the writing of the prophets are read as long as time permits. Then, when the reader has ceased, the president verbally instructs and exhorts to the imitation of these good things. Then we all rise together and pray, and, as we said before, when our prayer is ended, bread and wine are brought, and the president in like manner offers prayers and thanksgivings according to his ability, and the people assent, saying Amen. There is a distribution to each, and a participation in that over which thanks have been given, and to those who are absent a portion is sent by the deacons. And they who are well-to-do and willing to do so give what each thinks fit. What is collected is deposited with the president, who gives help to the orphans and widows, and to those who through illness or any other cause are in want, and to those who are in bonds, and to the strangers among us, and to all who are in need.

The third description comes from the defence of Christianity by Tertullian (c. AD 155–222), a Roman lawyer, who became a Christian as a result of being involved in prosecuting Christians and being affected by the reality and transparency of their faith and testimony. He writes:

We meet together as an assembly and congregation, in order that, offering up prayers to God as with united force, we may wrestle with Him in our supplications. This violence God delights in. We pray, too, for the Emperors, for their ministers, and for all in authority, for the welfare of the world, for the prevalence of peace, for the delay of the final consummation.

We assemble to read our sacred writings, if any peculiarity of the times makes either forewarning or reminiscence needful. However it be in that respect, with the sacred words we nourish our faith, we animate our hope, we make our confidence more steadfast; and, no less, by inculcation of God's precepts we confirm good habits. In the same place also exhortations are made, rebukes and sacred censures are administered. For with a great gravity is the work of judging carried on among us, as befits those who feel assured that they are in the sight of God; and you have the most notable example of judgment to come, when anyone has sinned so grievously as to require his severance from us in prayer, and the meeting and all sacred intercourse.

The tried men of our elders preside over us, obtaining that honour not by purchase, but by established character . . .

On the monthly collection day, if he likes, each puts in a small donation, but only if it be his pleasure, and only if he is able; for there is no compulsion, all is voluntary. These gifts are, as it were, piety's deposit fund. For they are not taken thence and spent on feasts and drinking bouts, and eating-houses, but to support and bury poor people, to supply the wants of boys and girls destitute of means and parents, and of old persons confined now to the house; such too as have suffered shipwreck; and if there happen to be any condemned to the mines, or banished to the islands, or shut up in prisons for their fidelity to the cause of God's Church, they become the nurslings of their confession.

He then speaks expansively of the Love Feast—a communal meal which every Christian shared on the Lord's

Day. Those who had plenty brought plenty, and those who had little brought little. Master and slave shared in the reality of fellowship, with the slave bringing often nothing but his hunger.

> Our feast explains itself by its name . . . The Greek word means love . . . As it is an act of religious service, it permits no vileness or immodesty. The participants before reclining taste first of prayer to God. As much is eaten as satisfies the craving of hunger; as much is drunk as befits the chaste. They talk as those who know that the Lord is one of their hearers. After they have washed, and after the lights have been brought in, each is asked to stand forth and sing, as he can, a hymn to God, either one from the Holy Scriptures, or one of his own composing . . . As the feast began with prayer, so with prayer it is closed. We go from it, not like troops of mischiefdoers, nor bands of roamers, not to break out in licentious acts, but to have as much care of our modesty and chastity as if we have been at a school of virtue rather than a banquet.

Certain features emerge from these descriptions that give us some clue as to how the early Christians used their liberty in Christ and so behaved on a Sunday. They clearly used the day for the study of the Scriptures, for prayer, for fellowship, for praise, for expressing social responsibility and concern, and for strengthening the moral fibre and resilience of life. They were free to give the whole day to God and to one another.

If you really love someone it never enters your head to say: 'How much time do I have to spend with my fiancée?' Quite the reverse is true: 'How much time can I spend with my fiancée and yet be honourable and responsible so far as the rest of life is concerned?' So with our relationship with God, its quality and reality can be determined by the amount of time and the attitude I adopt in wanting to be with Him in a conscious way and with His people in a practical way. It no longer is a question of, 'What is the minimum number of times I have to go to church?' or 'How much time do I have to spend in church?' (NB Not in the building, but with God's people!). I want to be as free as I can to give as much time to God as I can. I recognise I have other responsibilities, but here is a day when, by and large, I am free from these other responsibilities. Our attitude will be, 'Lord, I would love to spend every day like this with you and with those who clearly really love you, but there is other work to do and I have a responsibility to do it, but thank you for this one day'.

Our activity on Sunday is determined by our attitude of heart. Sunday is intended to be a foretaste of heaven. To reinstate its significance in our lives may well mean radical adjustments of our life-styles, our attitudes and our activities. The way we spend Sunday can often be far from the way God intended, and yet if we are going to experience the reality of the good life it will need to become a key feature.

6

Respect – like charity – begins at home

In 1861 the American Consul, John Howard Payne, died in Tunis. His consulate has long been forgotten; the plays he wrote are considered obsolete; his name does not stir the memory; but one of his poems has remained immortal – *Home; sweet home*. Children have learned to play it in their first piano lessons; sentimental vocalists have used it as their party piece; good men may have dismissed its heavy sentimentality, but endorsed its fundamental sentiment. A good home is fundamental to the good life. So says the Bible – and so says history! The Fifth Commandment lays down the first principle of a good home – respect for parents. Respect will need to be earned by the parents in order that they will be honoured by their children.

Significantly the Ten Commandments were originally divided into two tablets. The first includes the four Commandments which deal with man's relationship to God. The second tablet lists six Commandments which deal with man's relationship to his fellow man. In the broadest terms the Commandments teach us two basic lessons. The first is: if you want to live a good life pay attention to relationships. The good life does not in essence consist of what I possess or how much I achieve, but how I relate – to God and to man.

The home is the first classroom where we learn the primary lessons in good human relationships. If you don't get on with people in the home it will not be surprising that you don't get on with people elsewhere. The tragedy of what happened in the Garden of Eden is not simply that man ruined his natural and, until then, his inevitable fellowship with God, but he also ruined his needed and, until then, his uninhibited relationship with people. Genesis 4 follows naturally on Genesis 3. The triumph of what happened on the hill of Calvary is not simply that man was able at last to find fellowship with God, but also that he was able at depth to find relationships with man. All of this is authenticated in the Ten Commandments – get the vertical relationship right and the horizontal relationships will follow. Unhappily our society no longer believes this to be true. What God has joined together – religion and relationships – man has put asunder. This great divorce has soiled history through the years and millions have died as a result. To walk away from and despise God's order is a costly business. So these two areas are brought together in the Ten Commandments. Recognition of and response to God automatically affects the reality and resilience of our relationships with people. The home is where God intends us to begin. It is tragically easy within our society to be more concerned for those who live in the Third World than for those who sit across the table from us at breakfast time.

The home-life of Jesus makes powerful reading as it is recorded in Luke 2:39–52. In the 'silent years' of our Lord the only information we have is His attitude towards His parents and the resulting atmosphere in the home which they had established. God made flesh did not make light of parents, home and family. Here is a Commandment which goes right through into the New Testament without alteration or comment. As we have seen, some of the Commandments, as they pass through Jesus, are heightened, deepened and widened in their interpretation and implication, and although they are never dismissed, but rather endorsed by Him, they are also radically transformed. A good example is the Fourth Commandment which requires fulfilment in a different way by the Christian than by the Jew. The Fifth Commandment, however, is quoted verbatim six times in the New Testament – Matthew 15:14; 19:19; Mark 7:10; 10:19; Luke 18:20; and Ephesians 6:2. So it goes straight through from Jewish into Christian life. Whatever culture, education, civilisation, social and political pressure do to family life this Commandment remains unchanged. The size of families may change quite radically, but this Commandment remains. Certainly in the Western world, but also elsewhere today, an average family would have two or three children. Political pressure sometimes has reduced it lower than that. My mother-in-law, brought up within the security and simplicity of a Scottish village, was one of ten children, all of them ultimately doing very well for themselves in adult life and living to a ripe and robust old age (apart from one).

Another change which has taken place – especially within our Western culture – is that most homes today have only two generations living together (parents and children). Even within my life-time there used to be three generations living together. Children were as much influenced by grandparents as by parents because they were not only living nearby, but often were a physical part of the family unit. To ask if family life is better today as a result of this change is difficult to answer. At this time the number of people who live past the minimum pensionable age (between 60 and 65) is already much greater than ever before, and seems set now to continue to grow. In 1911 the proportion of these older people in the population was one in fifteen. By 1951 it had become two in fifteen. By 1977 the figure was three in fifteen. So in forty years it had doubled and then in twenty years the same increase had occurred. This trend continues with increasing rapidity.

The sex of children can now be secured. Testing the sex of an unborn child gives virtually 100 per cent recognition. Mothers are asking for an abortion so that they can have the kind of families they choose – all boys or all girls or one of each. The implications of this morally and socially leave great confusion behind.

Another powerful factor radically affecting the family is divorce: in 1979 one marriage was contracted every 85 seconds, but one divorce was secured every 180 seconds. The total number of divorcees in the United Kingdom alone is well in excess of two million, which indicates an increase of 600 per cent in the last twenty-five years – one of the highest increases in the Western world. One of the results is that over a million children are now in one-parent families. Significantly in 1850 only 4 per cent of British marriages were contracted in a registrar's office, but the notable year was 1977 when that percentage had risen to 51 per cent. The erosion of the Christian understanding of the sanctity and permanence of marriage has been widely replaced by a non-Christian assault on the traditional concepts of sex, marriage and the family. It is now confidently predicted that family life as we have known it will cease to be. Dr Jack Dominian, in a letter to *The Times* (14th July, 1983) wrote:

> Society is now witnessing a profound change in the nature of marriage. The name remains the same, but its inner world is changing from being primarily a permanent contract, in which the children and their welfare were its main concern to a relationship, intended to be permanent, in which companionship, equity and personal fulfilment are becoming just as important as the welfare of children.

George and Nena O'Neill go much further in their book *Open Marriage: A New Lifestyle for Couples* and confidently declare that monogamous marriage is obsolete, and urge their readers to replace an 'archaic, rigid, outmoded, oppressive, static, decaying, Victorian institution with one that is free, dynamic, honest, spontaneous, and creative'.

So it is that family life conceived in the heart of God and partially protected by the Fifth Commandment is breaking down. Two world wars (1914–1918 and 1939–1945) have both contributed to this process. Father was taken away and mother was left to cope as both father and mother. Then during World War II, in order to safeguard the future, children were evacuated without choice and the confusion and disintegration of family life was accelerated. In all of this parental roles became blurred. In the 1980s the incidence of massive unemployment has further contributed to the divine order being upset. 'It is the responsibility of both partners in a marriage to see that husband and wife roles do not become confused.' So writes Larry Christensen in *The Christian Family*. 'Men have been guilty of abdicating their role as head of the home, as women have been of usurping it. It is not easy to remain submissive to one who palms off his responsibilities upon you, and refuses to take the lead in family affairs.

'The emancipation of women has brought many needed reforms, but it has had the unfortunate side-effect of robbing women of securities and protection which are their right. Women today are put upon to shoulder financial problems and worries in the family, to spearhead civic programmes, to take the lead in raising the children, to represent the family to the community, to make major family decisions, to be the spiritual leader in the family. All of this is contrary to Divine Order. A woman is not normally equipped by nature to sustain this kind of psychological and emotional pressure and still fulfil her God-appointed role as wife and mother. The fact that women can do some of these things with technical competence only camouflages the irreparable damage – to women, to family, to society – of this departure from Divine Order.'

God knows nothing of a 50–50 marriage. God is looking for a 100–100 marriage where the man is 100 per cent man, husband and father and the woman is 100 per cent woman, wife and mother. It is only the debunking of God and the secularisation of society that has caused the necessity of determining and then defending women's (and indeed men's) rights.

Another factor in the whole scene which has added enormously to the confusion is the whole question of resources. Economic tightness plus an expectation of a standard of living which is exceptionally high – for all of us many luxuries have become necessities – has led to the working wife. I do not doubt that in some cases it may well be a fundamental necessity, but unhappily the exception has become the rule. Identity is dependent on activity – and the huge and demanding task of home-making does not rate very high in anybody's scale of values and thinking. The working wife is not only socially acceptable, but socially expected and, in some cases, insistently demanded. Her working life will span the time after marriage, during the children's childhood (their needs often intruding into the job security and advancement) and after the children have flown the nest. Humanist philosophy has done a sound job in robbing our society of a basic means of stability and richness here. I feel strong anger within me when I hear a woman introduce herself apologetically among her peer group with, 'I'm afraid I am only a housewife!' Strength has become weakness; importance and dignity have become triviality; superiority has become inferiority; and God's order has surrendered to man's confusion.

It needs to be said in this whole area that children often have more education, qualifications and wages than their parents. The result is that they become independent quickly, and so can often walk out of the home situation whenever something occurs which does not suit them.

I sense that behind all this, and so much more, Satan is rubbing his hands. Marriage, home and family life have always been a prime target of his. He knows – and we are so slow to learn after all the centuries and civilisations – that when family life is destroyed then the whole fabric of society quickly disintegrates. The result is confusion and insecurity, and Satan feeds on both!

This chapter on the relationship of the family to the good life will have achieved a vast amount if it only causes us to pause for a moment and consider where we are at personally, either as parents or as children. The question is not whether it suits me or my children/parents, but is my attitude and activity of such a kind that God is pleased with me here?

The same instruction occurs in Leviticus 19:3 as in Exodus 20:12: 'Each of you must respect his mother and his father . . .' in a slightly different form. The Jewish rabbis were quick to spot the difference that in Leviticus 'mother' comes first and they laboured the point to indicate that respect for both must be the same. 'It is known that a son naturally honours his mother more than his father, because she pets him. Therefore God put the honour of father before that of mother. It is known to God that a son reverences his father more than his mother, because his father teaches him the Law. Therefore God put the reverence of mother before that of father.' The rabbis insisted that the double form of the commandment existed to ensure the equal respect of both. Whether this is in fact the reason does not alter the fact that the conclusion of that teaching is true.

The importance of the Fifth Commandment can be seen in that it is the first commandment given after the first four commandments which affirm our duty to God and that the penalty for breaking it is death (Exod 21:17 and Lev 20:9). This is the same penalty as that for using blasphemy against God (Lev 24:15). There are two references to the Fifth Commandment in the Book of Proverbs (20:30 and 30:17). Both are awesome in their implications.

In view of all this, how do we honour and respect parents? What does it mean in practical terms? In view of the development in this relationship – as in any other – it will mean different things at different stages. In the *first* stage, while a child is at home and dependent on parents, respect will involve obedience. This will involve *complying* with the parents' decisions, directions and demands. From the earliest years everyone of us has wanted to be independent and manage our own lives. There is something within us which resents authority and struggles with submission to it. One of the lessons which needs to be learned early is that submission to authority does not normally restrict freedom, but liberates us into freedom. Nowhere can this be better learned than within the warmth, security and love of the home and family. I know that authority can be abused by those who exercise it, but this does not alter the fact that God intended that early in life we should learn how to handle and respond to authority. After all, in the end, to exercise authority properly and creatively will require that we know how to respond to it ourselves – this is God's divine order, and part of His prescription for the good life. Man's abuse of something good does not negate the purity and relevance of the divine intention. God always intended that the child must believe that his parents' love will never ask him to do anything but what is for his good. With the passage of the years the child will need to come to the understanding that not only does the parents' store of experience of life give them the right to offer guidance and advice, but also this is God's order for both parents and children. In the New Testament the directive is clearly given: 'Children, it is your Christian duty to obey your parents, for this is the right thing to do . . .' (Eph 6:1). Notice that the Bible doesn't give instructions to obedience when *they* are right, but rather the ground for obedience is that *this* is right. The responsibility for judging the rightness or otherwise of the parents' directions and instructions is not in the hands of the child, but firmly in the hands of the parent. This is an overwhelming parental responsibility. Any parent worthy of his task before God will not abuse this in a dictatorial or tyrannical way. He cannot in simple justice demand from the child any standard of conduct which he does not himself fulfil. Credibility is always at risk when we order others to do anything that we ourselves are not prepared to do. In any case any worthy parent will always be trying to build up in his child that proper independence which will enable that child to stand on his own feet and to face life on his own. As well as exercising control over a child a responsible parent will always regard his child as a person and have profound respect for this. The great and difficult task of parenthood is to exercise control in such a way that in the end the child will not need it any more. The fact remains, however, that the first stage in showing respect to parents is submission to their authority and compliance with their wishes and directions.

The *second* stage in showing respect for parents will change from *compliance* to *courtesy*. The second stage is marked by the change from dependence to independence. One of the difficulties faced by our society is that knowledge has poured out in the last thirty years or so in an unprecedented way. Young people today are in possession therefore of many more facts than their parents normally are. It is not every parent who is able to keep abreast of this knowledge explosion. This is compounded in today's society by the fact that contemporary young people have much better opportunities to learn than their parents had. For example, after the War the Barlow Report recommended that the number of university students should be doubled. This proposal has subsequently been found to be inadequate to meet the need. This enormous increase in educational opportunity has been made possible out of public funds rather than as a result of private means. I am a first-generation student (my parents did not have the opportunity to have a university education), but my family have had significantly more opportunities and facilities educationally than I had. Although restrictions are now being applied because of economic pressures which are being felt in every aspect of society, nevertheless it remains true that the scope of our children's knowledge continues to expand at a most remarkable pace. However, although our children may be cleverer than their parents (and what parent has not been somewhat stunned by his child's agility and expertise in handling a computerised watch or a calculator?) they are not necessarily wiser. This confusion between cleverness and wisdom can make some young people guilty of the very worst kind of snobbery – they look down on their parents. It is only the passage of the years and the experience of life which teaches you wisdom. If you intend to go on a journey to some specific part of the country it is always interesting to listen to what a geography student has to say about that particular terrain or what a history student has to say about the influence of the distant years on that area or an economics student's account of why it is industrial or rural, but if you want to get to your destination it is best to listen to the man who has himself travelled the road and so has personally experienced the dangers and the difficulties of travelling there. So it is with life.

What can so easily seem to the child to be narrow-mindedness in the parent is so often the desire by the parent for the child to have the best possible life. It is a curious fact of life that the things parents often insist on most strongly come from the parents' personal experience of situations where they have made mistakes themselves, were ignorant of the facts when they were coping with the reality, and subsequently had the deepest regrets at the way they either mishandled or completely failed at that point in their own lives. Often the hardest thing for children to understand is that parents want their children to learn the easy way from their experience rather than have to learn the hard way through their own mistakes and failures.

In this *second* stage then respect will be demonstrated by genuinely listening to and considering honestly what parents have to say about a situation with courtesy and humility. This needs to be real and not patronising. Children need to be convinced that no matter how many years they have spent at college and university, and no matter how many qualifications or degrees they may have secured, their parents' real, and sometimes painful, experience of life has made them just a little bit wiser than they are. Children also need to recognise that the anxiety that parents often display is a genuine concern to help the children to avoid some of the regrets they have as a result of the way they handled a comparable situation years before.

It is always an ugly thing when a parent holds over his child's head what he has done for him – it is in the realm of blackmail. The simple truth is that it is both a legal and a moral duty for a parent to provide for, care for, support and nourish his child. When a parent has done that he has done no more than his duty at whatever level and in whatever way that duty has been implemented. Occasionally I have known a parent with a grown child quite overtly to pressurise that child with the facts of how much has been done for him and been given to him during his growing years and that consequently he has a responsibility and right to be grateful and he will demonstrate his gratitude in doing or not doing according to the parent's wishes. I have known many more parents who have implied it by their attitude and reactions. This is despicable parental behaviour (however true the facts may be!). Nothing can justify it from the parents' side, since parents exist for their children and not the other way round. However, having said all that, a child does owe the parent his life in a double sense of the term. He owes him his life through birth, but he also owes him his life in that the parent cared for him and provided for him in the days and the years when he could not care and provide for himself, and when, if he had been left to himself, he would certainly have perished, and a human being's period of helplessness lasts for longer than that of any animal. A recognition of this should always encourage courtesy and respect by the child for the parent—albeit it will always be spontaneous and voluntary, and never never imposed and demanded.

The *third* stage of showing respect for parents will come towards the end of their lives, and *compliance* and *courtesy* will be replaced by a genuine and practical *caring*. Here the roles are reversed, and that is always a difficult change to make with humility. From being those who have basically supported their children, parents become those who need to be cared for and supported by their children. All kinds of emotions, tensions and often difficulties are part of this stage. The big question is not really, 'What shall we do?' but 'What would be the very best for my parents?' The answer is seldom the easiest or the most difficult solution which presents itself.

We have responsibility, as a church, for a home for the elderly directly across the road from our present church building where we care for 54 elderly people in three different forms of accommodation. These questions are not at all academic, therefore, but intensely practical and sometimes painful. Questions like, 'Should they move near to us?' 'Should they move in with us?' 'Should we look for protected accommodation for them?' 'What about their friends and familiar surroundings if we were to encourage them to move from where they are?' 'What about their dignity and sense of independence?' These are easy questions to ask, but it is very difficult to arrive at an accurate answer. It needs to be said that there is no easy answer and the right answer will differ in different people and at different times. As ever, it is always easier for us to give an answer to these questions when we are viewing someone else's situation than when we are actually and personally confronted with these questions. The answer will be found not in following always the easiest, most obvious and simplest way for me, but in honestly and honourably considering what is best and most fulfilling for them. Let nothing be done out of a sense of guilt or by yielding to peer-group pressure. I have serious problems with the person who generalises and makes bold statements about this whole area from a limited experience and often with a lack of personal involvement. It is my experience that heart-break and many tears from both parents and children are often the accompaniment of this particular stage.

To have respect for parents requires the same attitude always, but the expression of that attitude will change with the passage of the years and the circumstances which prevail at any particular stage. We have a very good example of all these stages in the earthly life of our Lord Jesus Christ. While He was a little child in the home of Mary and Joseph at Nazareth His attitude and resulting activity was one of compliance with the wishes of his parents. Little is known about the detail of these years although some bizarre traditional stories have emerged. We do know, however, that even though He was the

Son of God He was still subject to and obedient to the village carpenter and his wife (Luke 2:41–52). We do not know whether Mary or Joseph had discussed His origin with Him. We do not know whether Mary and Joseph shared with most other parents the awareness of their imperfection and the consequent mistakes they made in rearing Him. We do know, however, that His growth and development as a little boy was marked by His willing obedience to them.

The next stage is exemplified in that well-known incident at Jerusalem, where the boy of twelve assumed that His earthly parents accepted His independence, for He did not tell them where He was going. A Jewish boy became a man at the age of twelve, not eighteen or twenty-one. So Jesus' action was neither careless nor discourteous. A boy became a partner in his father's business at the age of twelve. This was normal, accepted and expected custom. Jesus gently reminds His parents of this during the events of this incident. However, even so, He was still obedient to Mary and Joseph (Luke 2:51). Even though He accepted His independence He was still submissive. The result of this submissive attitude while involved in an independent activity was that He grew in wisdom (not cleverness!) and He knew favour not only with God, but also with man. In other words this enabled Him to develop a good relationship with His Father in heaven and also with people on earth – presumably this included His father on earth! Those who want to rebel and dismiss God's order for living our lives within a family and as part of a fellowship will not enjoy good relationships either with God or with men. Jesus did not rebel, but expressed His respect for His parents in a practical way and so His life in the earthly family and with heavenly fellowship matured and developed.

The third stage of respect for parents is demonstrated on the *Cross*. Tradition has it that Joseph had died fairly early on in the Nazareth family's life – and that might well be true. Whether this is the case or not, Mary is alone by the time Jesus is hung on the Cross. He is aware that His mother is about to lose her son, and in that society her shelter and security would from then on be in jeopardy. Jesus never calls Mary His mother publicly. The term 'woman' is a title of deference and honour and respect. It is a powerful thing to realise that one of the last things Jesus did, while dying in a peculiar form of humiliation and agony when He might excusably have been totally preoccupied with His own intense pain, was to be concerned to make provision for His mother. Significantly this was taken care of by the disciple who was closer to Jesus during His earthly life than any of the other disciples – John. Having secured this care for His mother His life could now be given up to His heavenly Father.

We have looked at the Fifth Commandment mainly from the point of view of the reaction and relationship of children to parents. However, every relationship has two sides, and it would be important to consider this commandment from the other side – the attitude and activity of parents to children. The question needs to be asked of parents – are you honourable? Are you worthy of the respect which is being asked for? This should have no bearing on the children in their attitude and response to their parents, but it is a very important issue so far as parents are concerned. Do you make it easy for your children to disregard and despise you? How can you be a parent honoured and respected by your children?

First of all, and particularly in the *first* stage of the relationship, where the children are still at home and dependent, you need to be realistic and reasonable in the directions you give and the demands that you make. You need to take care to understand the child whom you are parenting, otherwise your expectations and requirements for that child are apt to be selfish, silly and arbitrary. If you are not understanding, then you will inevitably act in an irresponsible and unreasonable way. There are too many homes today in which parents and children are almost strangers to each other – the parent has nothing of any real significance to say to the child. Some parents find it easier to communicate with those outside their own family rather than with their own children. This is an unmitigated tragedy.

Of course the cleavage between one generation and the next is no new thing. To review history is quickly to be made aware of this. There is a well-known verdict of one generation on another:

> The world is passing through troublous times. The young people of today think of nothing but themselves. They have no reverence for parents or old age. They are impatient of all restraint. They talk as if they knew everything, and what passes for wisdom with us is foolishness with them. As for the girls, they are forward, immodest and unwomanly in speech, behaviour and dress.

That has a contemporary ring about it, but it is an extract from a sermon (why can sermons be so pompous!) preached by Peter the Hermit in 1274. Clearly his generation never really understood the generation which followed it. Undoubtedly, the largest part of responsibility for this estrangement must lie at the door of the older generation. On the whole older people find it difficult to take on board in their thinking that things have changed, time has passed, and life has moved on. Life is never content to stand still – and we need to acknowledge that, otherwise we will find ourselves living in an unreal world. Nowhere will an unwillingness to recognise this be sadder or more destructive than in the living relationship of one generation with another. Elinor Mordaunt, the novelist, will not be the first parent to say to her child: 'I would never have been allowed to do that when I was your age'. On the face of it, and in the cold light of day, it is a pretty useless piece of information anyway. To that comment Elinor Mordaunt's daughter replied: 'But you must remember, mother, that you were then and I'm now'. Just so – it is the then and the now which causes all the trouble. The parent may judge that things have not developed for the better with the passage of a generation – but that should only make him more sympathetic and understanding of his child. One generation is different from another generation, for better or for worse, and the biggest step to understanding on both sides will be that parents ought not to expect their children to be the same as themselves and vice versa. This is not totally to exonerate the younger generation, for impatience and intolerance are characteristics of youth in all generations including our own, but it is the responsibility of those who are older – and supposedly more mature – to exercise the patience which will keep the lines of communication and understanding open between the generations. Respect will be gained by recognising and honouring this.

Secondly at the stage where children are now largely independent and free from parental support the parents need to be positively willing to release them and to relinquish their control over them. This *second* stage, to be constructive, will have to be done gradually, but nevertheless it must be done. Most parents have struggled here, for they find it difficult to come to terms with the fact that their child is no longer the child that they have known over many years. He is now a young adult in his own right. He has views that are worth listening to (even though they may differ from the parents). He has convictions which are deeply held and often dearly won. He can do some things often much better than the parent can. He has standards and values by which he wants to live his life just as the parent has. In other words he is a person – and as such needs to be regarded as an intelligent human being. Respect and courtesy will only be earned when a parent recognises this and willingly lets his child go, rather than trying by one means or another to keep him under his control. There is always the constant pressure, in perfectly normal circumstances, of the child wanting to be an adult too quickly, but equally the parent adds to this pressure by wanting to keep the adult as a child too long.

Jesus tells a remarkable story of a son who said to his father, 'I want my share of your estate now instead of waiting until you die!' The father 'agreed to divide his wealth between his sons' (Luke 15). Painful though it was he released his son. In spite of all the anguish that caused the father (and indeed the son!) he did not lose his son. I remember years ago two missionaries sitting in our living room sharing with us how their son, who had done well at university and qualified in his chosen profession with great distinction, claimed that he had been converted from Christianity and gone into his 'far country'. The pain and hurt of both these parents was not hard to see. As we sat chatting the father said, 'It has been a great comfort and strength to us to remember that in Jesus' story of the Prodigal Son the father did not go into the far country to look for him or interfere with him. He simply waited and watched, and the moment his head appeared over the horizon there was a warm and sincere welcome waiting for him'. In this case the parents, after many anxious years, did have the joy of seeing their son 'come home'. It may not be so for all, but the parental responsibility remains – release your child to be the man or woman of tomorrow! On that same evening these two missionaries said to Anne and me, 'Isn't it strange how as Christians we commit our children in our prayers into the Lord's hands and then proceed to behave as if we really believed they were in the devil's hands.' Point taken.

Thirdly, a new stage is reached which for the parents – and often for the children – is the most difficult of all. This *third* stage is signalled when children have to change roles with the parents. Children ultimately will have to adopt the role of supporters rather than supported. Deep human emotions are involved here on both sides. Exposure and vulnerability are inevitable accompaniments. The pride and independence of the parents are the hardest factors to cope with. Sensitivity and patience are required by the children and humility and grace are required by the parents. Managing this stage is never easy for either. It certainly is more blessed to give than to receive, but it is much more difficult to receive than to give. Having given so willingly, and for so many years, reversing the roles is intensely difficult. However difficult, this third stage needs to be worked out and worked through.

Crucial to living the good life is this respect for a practical relationship with parents. Some have even felt that the Fifth Commandment should be included with the first four – since it relates more to our relationship with God than to our relationship with people. This is quite understandable since honouring and respecting parents is a vital ingredient in our relationship with God. Those who do not respect their earthly father will have real difficulty in knowing how to respect their Father in heaven. It has become an increasing problem in the United Kingdom that many now grow up in an earthly family where there is often only one parent – and the missing parent is the father. Lack of experience of having, and then relating to, an earthly father has its effect in relating to our heavenly Father. At the same time the pressure of life and the extraordinary strains that come upon marriages create strange anomalies in parenting. Our experience in counselling at the church has helped us to recognise that where the earthly father is weak, distrust, insecurity and apprehensiveness of the heavenly Father will result. Where the earthly father is strong and domineering, fear, resentment and an unhealthy cringing before the heavenly Father will result. This is not the place to discuss the full implications of the strength or weakness of this human and natural relationship upon the spiritual relationship and attitude towards God. Suffice it to say, however, from the child's point of view that learning to respect and honour parents through the different stages will help enormously in our honour, respect and trust towards God.

Perhaps the last word of this chapter should be to parents rather than to children. I can remember sitting in a lovely home in Minneapolis enjoying being part of a family for a day while I was so far away from my own family. That family had known great tragedy. One day some years before, all had been straightforward and normal and family life was proceeding in a somewhat humdrum way. Lance (not his real name) had a key job, and a dangerous one, with one of the large American airlines and earned well. He had literally built the house which was now their home and had incorporated many lovely features into it, including a fine swimming pool. He was working around the house on this day and had gone to get some chemicals for the swimming pool. In the few minutes it took him to do this his little girl had gone to the pool, where he had been working, looking for him and had fallen in. No noise had been heard and the time factor was unbelievably short, but he returned to find her face down on the surface – dead. The marks of grief were still there, but the consequences of this bereavement had led Lance and his wife to adopt five children – each of different nationalities. I valued their conversation, and during supper Lance made many shrewd comments about being a parent. The one which struck me most and has remained with me over the years was his comment: 'The best way a father can love his children is to love their mother'. I believe that is true! I think that in the same way the best thing earthly parents can do for their children is to make sure that they have a living, personal relationship with their heavenly Father! Parents with a second-hand Christian experience will try to pass it on to their children and frankly it cannot be done. Too many parents today are trying to live an adult life with a childhood faith which lacks understanding, content, resilience, and often reality. The result is that the faith we hand on to our children is legalistic and formal – and often dead.

I note with unlimited joy that a new generation is rising which will be able to pass reality on to their children. For them loving and serving God is not a dull, formal duty any longer – but a delight. For them Sunday is no longer sombre and restrictive, but exciting and creative. For them Christian fellowship is not shallow and polite, but has life-transforming depths and is devastatingly real. In the midst of all the godlessness and declining values within our society this gives grounds for hope – and I find that exhilarating as I am well into the second half of my life.

However I am left wondering what my generation is really passing on to its children. Are we passing on a God who is seen and known to be able to do exceedingly abundantly? Are we passing on a God who meets badness with grace rather than with goodness? Are we passing on a God of justice as well as of mercy, who is quite unwilling to put up with anything for the sake of peace? Are we passing on a God who can be trusted absolutely in every situation however bewildering and confusing it might be to us? This is the parent's duty and joy, but he requires to find this dimension of reality himself before he can pass it on. Is there anything more important to seek and to find than this?

Paul (Eph 6:2) says that this is the first commandment with a promise attached to it. Clearly the promise is not carried on into the New Testament (see Matt 15:4 and 19:19; Mark 7:10 and 10:19; Luke 18:20 and Eph 6:2). However, although the blessing which accompanies the Fifth Commandment is not in a material dimension, clearly God intends to bless those who will keep it. Amidst all the fierce pressures amongst us and within us which would lead us to lack respect in so many ways, let us honour God by respecting our parents on earth and so enjoy the blessing of God and experience the good life for which He has created us and redeemed us.

7

Man's most precious possession of all

The death of a fellow human being no longer affects us deeply – unless we personally knew, respected and valued that person as an individual. Famine and disaster in a distant land cause little response – and the next programme on television soon absorbs us. Herr Willy Brandt, the former West German Chancellor, in 1980 gave his name to an investigation of North–South economic inequality and the report of the Brandt Commission burst on the scene under the title *North–South: A Programme for Survival.* Brandt describes North–South relations as 'the greatest challenge to mankind for the remainder of this century'. The Commission released evidence that 800 million people in our world are destitute, while although some real progress has been made in the Third World, every two seconds a child dies of hunger and disease. Criticism may be levelled at the Brandt Commission, but the facts which it presents ought to be deeply disturbing. By and large, frankly, they are not. At breakfast we read of an air crash in Yugoslavia. Everyone aboard was killed including seven children. But quickly we are scrutinising the sports page and how the Test Match is going. After all, as far as is known, there were no Britons on board – not that that would have made too much difference. By the end of 1986 it is estimated that there were 170,000 abortions in that year in the UK. The vast majority of these had nothing to do with the survival of the mother. Wholesale murder of defenceless children in the womb is occurring in our nation, and we accept it as part of the progress of our space-age generation. The local paper gives tragic detail of a car crash killing a local woman, with pictures of the twisted metal of the two vehicles involved – but then we did not know her. She and the accident become one more statistic for the Ministry of Transport and for someone doing a thesis on the production of cars or road development in the South-East of England.

My first experience of a funeral was as a young boy. My great-aunt had died. I did not know her very well although there was a family ritual in my earliest memories that on the first day of each year we visited her. I don't think we had much contact with her apart from this annual visit. I remember very little about her, apart from a magnificent collie dog she had called Glen, a grandfather clock that had four little dials inside the main clock-face which all worked at the same time and the blue china from which we had tea. On her death we all attended the funeral. It must have been important since I had to be suitably dressed for the occasion. However, the most important thing to me about that day was that I was assigned a seat to myself beside the driver of one of the magnificent black limousines which were in the funeral cortege. I never spoke to the driver and he never spoke to me. I didn't know what you were supposed to do at a funeral, so I sat and stared out of the window, mostly looking straight ahead, because everyone else seemed to be doing that. This funeral took place in one of Glasgow's suburbs in the middle of the day. Two things surprised and delighted me – the traffic moved over to allow us to pass and waited until we were well clear, and a soldier in full uniform saluted with military precision as the hearse passed him. He could not have been more dramatic had my great-aunt been royalty. That memory is as clear as on the day it happened. I have attended many funerals over the years – and often I've sat beside the driver of one of the limousines (talking to him now!) – but the other traffic now becomes restless and irritable at the hold-up and roars past as soon as there is space to do so. No one on the pavement seems to pay the slightest attention – well, maybe just occasionally – and no hats are raised or salutes given.

What is happening to us? There needs to be a revival of sensitivity. It is not enough for us not to murder. It is not enough not to hate. Before there can be brotherhood or love, there must be sensitivity to human suffering and grief. Evidence of insensitivity is all around us and the death of even one fellow human being – let alone many – has little, if any, effect on us. Were there to be a revival of sensitivity, perhaps we would see a rebirth of compassion. When we begin to be deeply disturbed and disquieted because there are human beings dying lonely and often callous deaths, perhaps we will really begin to care. To care is to be concerned, and concern is the first stirring of compassion. If there is compassion, men may still disagree strongly and deeply, but they will not be cruel and mean.

The Sixth Commandment forbids murder specifically, not killing in general. It establishes one fact very strongly – the sanctity of human life. The most important thing in human relationships is respect for human life. The respect for marriage, possessions and reputation, safeguarded in the following Commandments, is built on this foundation that human life is man's most precious possession. During the time of the Roman Empire, Varro, the Roman writer on agriculture, wrote a passage which seems grim and inhuman to us, but which seemed perfectly and inevitably natural to a Roman. He divided the instruments of agriculture into three classes – the articulate, the inarticulate and the mute: 'the articulate comprising the slaves, the inarticulate comprising the cattle, and the mute comprising the vehicles'. The only difference between a slave and a beast or a wagon is that the slave can talk. Cato, an older writer on agriculture, gives advice for the correct management of a farm and the putting into order of a farm which has been slackly administered. 'When slaves were sick, such large rations should not have been issued.' 'Look over the livestock and hold a sale. Sell your oil, if the price is satisfactory, and sell the surplus of your wine and grain. Sell worn-out oxen, blemished cattle, blemished sheep, wool, hides, an old wagon, old tools, an old slave, a sickly slave, and whatever else is superfluous.' The worn-out slave is classed with the broken tool and the beasts which are of no further use. When he ceases to be of use he is superfluous and is to be got rid of. All of this may seem to belong to a totally different civilisation from ours until you listen to the Reith Lecture given in 1967 by Dr Edmund Leach. During his lecture Dr Leach said, 'There is no sharp break in continuity between what is human and what is mechanical'. Raquel Welch, the film actress, in an article in a well-known national newspaper entitled 'The Torment of the World's Number One Sex Symbol', is reported to have said, 'I am just a piece of meat . . . I fulfil the ambitions of other people to make money out of me.' When you eliminate the difference between 'she' and 'it' and regard 'she' or 'he' simply as a means to an end – an object to be used – you create a whole range of serious problems. If there is no ultimate meaning to life then why get upset about injustice? Why protest about social and racial inequality? How can I be fair or unfair, just or unjust, to what is basically a machine?

C. S. Lewis has a chilling passage in which he writes:

She was beautifully, delicately made,
So still, so unafraid,
Till the bomb came.
Bombs are the same,
Beautifully, delicately made.

The Industrial Revolution brought into being a concept of workers whereby they were called 'hands'. We have gone a little further than that and spoken of 'heads' (i.e. per capita of the population) and we have given these 'heads' serial numbers. In the American University of Illinois, the College of Fine and Applied Arts has tried to humanise today's trend towards computerisation. Each term the administration sends out a card to check the student's programme. The accompanying letter begins something like this: 'Dear 344-28-0430: we have a personal interest in you . . .' Unhappily the reality mocks the sentiment. Depersonalisation is part of the philosophy of today, shared in particular by Marxists, nihilists (nihilism is the philosophy of total scepticism i.e. there is no meaning, no aim, no values, no purpose, no answer to the question why?), and the pushers of pornography. If Marx's dictum is true, that 'the material world to which we belong is the only reality', then anything goes. Dr Victor Frankl, who survived the Auschwitz concentration camp, says that the nihilistic philosophies of the nineteenth century led to the death camps of the twentieth century, and that even now there is a 'nihilist tendency to devalue and depreciate that which is human in man'. Whether for sex or violence, men and women often tragically use one another.

This Commandment is here to safeguard against this continually growing pressure of dehumanisation. The Sixth Commandment underscores a firm conviction that man was made in the image of God, and although that image is defaced, spoiled, stained and defiled – potentially it can still be restored by grace. This Commandment is about reverence for life and is intended to protect the sanctity of life. It is declaring that man is much more than a machine and that all human values, personal considerations, love, caring, sharing, compassion, justice, honesty and friendship are important. So we are not to be indifferent about Hitler's massacre of six million Jews or Stalin's murder of twenty million people.

The Sixth Commandment does pose the question: 'What do you mean by life?' Albert Schweitzer, the good and godly doctor and brilliant musician, who went to practise medicine in the unsophisticated environment and hostile climate of Lamberene in Africa at the call of God, took it to mean all biological life – plants and animals as well as humans. This caused immense tension in him and also in his work as a doctor. Plant life must be killed to sustain animal life and all humans live by eating food that was once living matter. The Sixth Commandment does not mean that life is never to be exterminated. There are those who will not, like Schweitzer, ever kill a mouse or a rat. They have a sentimental rather than a realistic opinion/conviction that all life is sacred, an emotional judgment that will not stand up in logic or in life. We kill rodents because we value the life of a man more than the life of a rat. Dr Schweitzer's refusal to kill vermin and insects created serious situations for the staff in the hospital at Lamberene. The Sixth Commandment is concerned with murder rather than killing in general. It is not concerned with plants and animals since these do not bear the image of God although they do indicate something of God's majesty in creation. This Commandment is concerned with reverence for human life.

Having firmly established this fact we can now lay down three areas where it is relevant. The Sixth Commandment first of all has a strong and obvious *personal* relevance. This is the basic area which it covers. It refers to the situation where one human being deliberately, wilfully and maliciously kills another human being. It is not addressed to society or the group, but to the individual. The grammar uses 'you' in the singular here. It would be easier, and certainly less controversial, to close our study of the Sixth Commandment here. However relevant this is it does not do justice to two other areas. As well as referring to the *personal* area it also refers to the *social* area of life. Each individual is part of a group. No man is an island and lives for himself. I, as an individual, have a responsibility with a group. Sometimes the group to which I belong takes upon itself the responsibility to kill. Many groups practise capital punishment as a form of punishment for certain crimes. As a member of the group I need to come to some conclusion about whether capital punishment is in fact a proper punishment or not. Sometimes also, the group to which I belong takes upon itself the responsibility to declare war on other groups to which others belong. As a member of the group I need to come to some conclusion about whether war is ever a valid means to settle some issues and preserve some values.

The third area of relevance of this commandment is *medical.* In our contemporary society we are struggling with two main contexts medically – at either end of life – birth and death. It is true that science can add years to our lives, but only Jesus Christ can add life to our years. It is true that science can offer a longer life to man, but it is equally true that science cannot offer a better life to man. Man can extend the quantity of life, but do little to alter the quality of life. Both abortion and euthanasia are powerful issues today. Facts and statistics are fairly easy to come by and the sheer numbers involved can often obscure the devastation and darkness inherent in them. Today, in western society, although it would be denied by many and obscured by the semantics of the matter, abortion is virtually available on demand. A former Archbishop of Canterbury in the mid-1970s spoke of it as 'a runaway bus' and 'a weapon of national suicide'.

Euthanasia, on the other hand, contains two aspects to its sinister trauma. There is 'soft' euthanasia which is practised when a life-support system is withdrawn from a badly injured or diseased body. In the 1970s America's first 'right to die' Bill was passed, amidst a great deal of controversy, by the State Assembly in California. It allowed terminally ill patients to order their doctors to put an end to artificial life-sustaining efforts. It met dogged opposition and was worded in such a way that its application would be very limited. This Bill was passed in the California Assembly by 43 votes to 25. It was prompted by the case of Karen Ann Quinlan, the New Jersey woman in a coma whose fate had to be decided in court. The Bill allows the 'right-to-die' directive to be signed by patients if they are witnessed by at least two people not related to the patient nor involved in the medical treatment. These documents would be considered valid for five years, but could not take effect for fourteen days after they are signed. The document would not be binding on the attending physician unless he and another doctor agreed that the patient was in an imminently terminal condition. The patient's doctor would also be under the obligation to decide whether the patient had been competent to make the decision when the document was signed. There are very wide provisions for the patient to have a change of mind, either verbally or in writing. With an eye to possible abuses, the Bill makes it illegal for any insurance company to require a 'right-to-die' document as a condition for providing medical insurance. It so happens that the catalyst in producing the Bill – the Karen Quinlan case – would not have been relevant to the Bill because Miss Quinlan lapsed into a coma after mixing drugs and alcohol and not through terminal illness.

There is a much more sinister aspect, however, to euthanasia – 'hard' euthanasia. This is the administering of drugs positively and deliberately to terminate life. Whether personally, socially, or scientifically it is important that we understand the implications and directions of the Sixth Commandment so that we can act and react in situations of this kind according to the will of God.

There are three different reactions to the situations which this commandment covers. First of all there is the *emotional* reaction – 'What do I feel about this situation?' In the area of capital punishment the question is often asked by those who resist and refuse capital punishment for any crime whatsoever – 'Would you ever put a rope round a man's neck with a view to breaking it?' The thought is so repulsive to most normal people that a negative response is inevitable. The logic is then affirmed that if you would not do it personally what right have you to ask another to do it on your behalf. In a rather different vein relating to war the question is often asked: 'Can you imagine Jesus releasing a bomb that killed 87,000 people in one second and blighted the lives of countless thousands of others?' (This was what happened when the first atomic bomb was dropped on Hiroshima in 1945.) In our hearts there is a strong negative response which struggles with great intensity with a passage like Revelation 5:1–6 where Jesus releases horrendous plagues and tragedies on earth such as the world has not yet seen. In other words, in both these situations, our hearts strongly say: 'I cannot imagine it!' whilst the Bible says: 'He is capable of it, and He will!' Our nation is divided down the middle, not so much by those who believe in God and those who do not. Our nation is divided by those who believe in one kind of God and those who believe in another kind of God. There are those who believe in a God who is a mixture of sentimentality, imagination, ignorance, and wishful thinking, and there are those who believe in the God of the Bible. When it comes to the life and death issues which this commandment deals with, 'What do I feel?' is not the right approach. Our emotions are important and very real, but sometimes can mislead us pretty badly.

Secondly, there is the *corporate* reaction – 'What do others or the majority think about this?' It is so easy to allow the spirit and the mood of the age to determine what course of action ought to be followed. In the England of John Wesley's day there were 160 crimes for which men, women, and children could be hanged. Today there are none. Were they wrong and we right? Society endorsed capital punishment in Wesley's day and society rejects capital punishment today. Is this a satisfactory way to determine what is right or wrong? The majority say so! The fact of the matter is that the commandments of God are not on approval by men – they are absolute not relative. There is no such thing as a new morality – only the old immorality. There are not things which are sometimes right and sometimes wrong. Once you disallow absolutes in morality you lose morals. There can be little doubt that we have come to an era where the sanctity of human life has deteriorated. The reason is not far to seek – we have moved away from God's way of thinking. We can blame the media; television entertainment; the demand for a rich life-style at the expense of many others; an obscene disregard for the destitute and the dying by the West – but at the heart of it all lies the fact that when you remove God from the scene the dehumanisation of man quickly follows. The implications of that are devastating. Lack of respect for human life is an inevitable accompaniment.

Thirdly, there is the *divine* reaction, 'What does God think about it?' We are faced with a difficulty here since there are many areas in our modern world where God has made no direct detailed pronouncement – and abortion and euthanasia are two of these areas. We are left to feel our way on issues like these. God has made direct pronouncements on some issues however – and capital punishment, war and murder are among them. It is much more secure to follow what God has already declared than to be influenced by the whim of our emotions or the fluctuating desires of one society or another.

However difficult it is for us, and however open it may leave us to misrepresentation and misunderstanding, it is important to apply the Sixth Commandment at a personal, social and medical level.

Clearly at a *personal* level deliberate, intentional, malicious murder is forbidden absolutely. It is important to affirm yet again that this commandment is dealing with murder in particular and not killing in general. God also makes a clear distinction between murder and manslaughter. The law of God, which is so stern in its demands, is astonishingly careful to preserve the rights of even a guilty man. The great danger to the person who killed another was that an enraged and grief-stricken next of kin might go after such a person and take his life in the spirit of a vengeful vendetta rather than a spirit of justice. To meet this kind of situation it was laid down that there should be in Israel six cities of refuge (Josh 20:1–9). These were to be so chosen and sited that every part of the country would have its city. So there were three cities on the west of the Jordan – Hebron in the Judaean mountains, Shechem in Mount Ephraim, and Kedesh in the hill country of Naphtali. There were three other cities of refuge in the east side of the Jordan – Bezer in the plain belonging to Reuben, Ramoth in Gilead in the territory of Gad, and Golan in Bashan in the territory of Manasseh. The roads to these cities were kept open and perhaps even, as it were, signposted, and it has been calculated that the cities were so distributed that no one could ever be more than thirty miles from one of them.

The object of these cities was that a man who had killed another might flee to one of them. There the circumstances of the killing could be properly investigated and in Exodus 21:12, 13; Numbers 35:6–34; Deuteronomy 4:41–43; 19:1–13; and Joshua 20:1–9 clear detailed guidelines are laid down. If the killing could be proved to have been accidental, if it came from a push or a blow or even a stab that was not meant to kill, if something had been thrown and had killed a man and there had been no intention of killing him, apparently even if the blow had been struck in a moment and in an excess of passion, then the killer was given refuge. The unintentional killer was tried by the elders. There is a clear distinction made by God between murder and manslaughter.

There are two things which emerge from the Bible about murder. First of all the Bible makes it clear that murder takes away from a man his most precious possession – his life. Having taken it from him, he can never get it back. This is the supreme robbery. Murder is wrong because it is sacrilege – it defaces and destroys something which has been made like God. To deface the Queen's image is a culpable offence within our society today. The most serious defacing of God's image is to murder. So the really serious thing about murder is that you are doing something to deface and destroy God's image (Gen 9:6). Murder is not simply doing something to man, but doing something to God. The animal and the plant – wonderfully made as they are – are not made in God's image. In touching man you are touching God's image.

The second interesting thing the Bible says about murder is that it defines how it is to be punished. It takes us beyond Moses and the Ten Commandments; beyond even Abraham, the father of the faithful; and back to the time of Noah. There a simple statement is made, 'Man was made like God, so whoever murders a man will himself be killed by his fellow-men' (Gen 9:6). The context is that God has already destroyed a whole society Himself and He is saying to Noah – 'If society is going to keep the sanctity of life intact the murderer has to lose his life'. From this beginning this affirmation goes on through the Bible. There are those who feel that the Sixth Commandment forbids capital punishment. However, it is necessary to go into the very next chapter of the book of Exodus where it says plainly: 'But when a man gets angry and deliberately kills another man, he is to be put to death, even if he has run to my altar for safety' (Exod 21:14). This really is the point on which the whole discussion hangs – you cannot simply quote proof texts to substantiate your conclusions, but rather look and see the whole sweep of revelation. If once you will grant capital punishment as valid and the will of God you will then have granted one thing – justice is even more important than human life. If human life is the highest value then you would not kill the murderer under any circumstances. But justice is above human life because God is just, and He has worked on this principle from the very beginning.

To say that capital punishment does not reform the criminal, or provenly deter other criminals, may well be quite true – but it misses the point. The foundational point about capital punishment for murder is that the divine image in man has been attacked and justice must be done and sustained.

At a *social* level the issues raised by the Sixth Commandment become even more emotive. Few people would doubt that in order to have an ordered and meaningful society law is necessary. Law is the foundation of society and also the cement which holds it together. Without law society would disintegrate altogether. It is law which protects the ordinary person against the person who is not only strong, but unscrupulous, selfish and evil in his intentions. Even in the ordinary everyday activities of life such as driving a car, building or buying a house, selling and buying, the observance of law is essential if life is to go on at all.

Human nature, however, being as it is, there will always be the desire to break the law. This will happen either carelessly or deliberately. The law must therefore provide itself with sanctions, and so punishment is necessary for the maintenance of that law, which is the basis of society. Punishment and law need to go hand in hand so that there may be a fitting penalty for law-breaking.

This is not to say that there may not sometimes be bad law, law which is partial rather than impartial, law which appears to favour one section of the community rather than the other. Nor is it to say that there will not be times when operating the law is patently unsatisfactory – when those who administer it are corrupt, or when its application is erratic and unpredictable. But in normal circumstances it is law which holds society together, and therefore for the sake of society any breach of it, or any defiance of it, must be punished.

It is in this *social* context that capital punishment and war particularly emerge. In a church where I was once the pastor the chief probation officer for the area was in the congregation. He passionately contended that capital punishment neither reformed the criminal nor deterred other criminals. The former is self-evident and he could substantiate the latter by statistics and by personal experience. However, as we have already seen, neither of these is quite the point. The point, as already indicated, is that in murder the divine image in man is being attacked, the sanctity of life is being destroyed, and justice must be maintained. Murder and theft cannot be treated in the same dimension – and the punishment must fit the crime.

With regard to war those who honourably hold a pacifist position would point out that the Church took the wrong turning in the fourth century when it allied itself with attitudes of the state and identified itself with wars. The pacifist would also be able to back up his argument from the earliest Christian writings. Here are two from the first century: Lactantius wrote with no embellishment, 'It is not lawful for a just man to engage in warfare'. Basil, from the same century, recorded that soldiers, after their discharge from the armed forces, were excluded from Communion for three years. Perhaps the most powerful conclusion in the pacifist's convictions is that the whole life of Jesus reflected an attitude of non-resistance and non-violence. 'He was treated harshly, but endured it humbly; he never said a word. Like a lamb about to be slaughtered, like a sheep about to be sheared, he never said a word' (Isa 53:7).

The non-pacifist on the other hand would counter with the fact that there is no known case of a man being refused baptism or admission into church membership on the grounds that he was a soldier. In fact there was a group of Christians in the Twelfth Legion of Marcus Aurelius which met regularly for prayer, and there was an Egyptian Legion in the third century which was acknowledged as being wholly Christian. It is true that there are conscientious objectors registered in the second century, but they were so for different reasons than pacifism. At that time the Roman Army involved each soldier in pagan ceremonies and the acknowledgment of the pagan gods on the festival days. It was in response to these practices that some felt unable by conscience to be part of the armed forces. The non-pacifist would point out that where justice was at stake – apart from his own redemptive, vicarious work on the Cross – Jesus was strong in action. A good example of this would be His teaching based on His observations and experience in Matthew 23.

The great danger in all of this is that of transferring the principle of personal ethics into a principle of national law and international relationships. The Rev. J. R. W. Stott observes: 'No war is justified to a biblical Christian unless it is a glorified police action to bring criminals to justice'. In other words where the members of society need to be protected, and what is good within society needs to be preserved, then it will be necessary and right for the state to use force. Clearly Christians are unable to accept that all war is right. However, the majority of Christians have never believed that all war is wrong. The clear biblical revelation is not that all war is right or that all war is wrong, but rather that *justice* is always right. Sometimes it may be necessary and right to use the ultimate sanction of physical force to maintain the principle and the reality of justice. All through the Bible that is what God does. The clear teaching of the Bible is that force is not to be used in the service of the heavenly kingdom, but it may be necessary in the service of the earthly society. The tension arises because Christians are citizens of both. We are required to render to Caesar what belongs to Caesar and to God what belongs to God.

The easiest course is to join the armed forces and fight any war we are told to fight. The more difficult course of action is to become a conscientious objector or to be prepared to join only the medical corps or some other non-combatant section of the armed forces. The most difficult course of action is to do neither of these two, but to be willing to fight when justice warrants it and to be willing not to fight when it doesn't.

At a *medical* level, never have the implications of the Sixth Commandment been more hotly debated. Within the context of abortion the crucial question is to decide when human life begins. The main divide lies between those who hold that a foetus is not a human being until it breathes independently and those who are convinced that human life begins at the time of conception. This controversy has put into everyone's understanding the wonderful process of human gestation.

From *day 1*, when conception takes place as the sperm and the ovum meet in fertilisation, the genetic make-up of the child is complete. Thc colour of the eyes and the hair, the sex and even the build of the child are determined. In other words a unique individual is present in the womb.

By *day 17* the new child is developing its own blood cells, and the placenta is now established.

By *day 20* the foundation of the entire complicated and intricate nervous system is established.

By *day 21* the heart starts to beat, and this is at least as dramatic as birth.

By *day 30* there is a regular blood flow within the closed vascular system. The ears and the nose start to develop.

By day 42 the skeleton is complete in detail and reflexes are now present. The liver, kidneys and lungs are now formed.

By *day 43* the electrical brain wave patterns can be recorded.

By *day 56* all organs are functioning; growth and maturity are all that occur now, in the same way that a child grows into an adult.

By *day 65* the baby can make a fist and grasp an object stroking his palm. The baby will now be able to leap up and down in the womb with movements co-ordinated.

By *week 16* the baby is half birth-length and its heart pumps 50 pints of blood daily.

By *week 20* the hair appears on the head.

By *week 28* the eyes are open. The baby can hear the mother's digestive processes and heartbeat. For some time social abortions could be legally performed in Britain until this time had elapsed according to the Infant Life (Preservation) Act 1929.

By *week 36* birth would be normal—just another stage in a well-advanced process.

It is quite clear that from a very early stage the baby can feel pain. From the above it is purely an arbitrary matter to pass a law affirming that at so many weeks it is legal to abort and after that it becomes illegal. In spite of the contemporary controversy among Christians (opposing views often genuinely and honourably held) Christian tradition has from the time of the early Church been firmly against anything that might undermine the sacredness of human life, including that of the unborn child. The Didache, one of the earliest known Christian writings for instructing Christians outside the New Testament, clearly says: 'Thou shall not kill the foetus in the mother's womb'.

In modern times both Protestants and Catholics have re-affirmed this view, although Catholics have probably been the most faithful to it. Pope John Paul II, speaking in Ireland in 1979 said,

> So I say to all, have an absolute and holy respect for the sacredness of human life from the first moment of its

> conception. To attack unborn life at any moment from its conception is to undermine the whole moral order which is the true guardian of the well-being of man. The defence of the absolute inviolability of unborn life is part of the defence of human rights and human dignity.

The same view was put forward by Protestants in Scotland:

> Though poles apart in vital doctrine from the Church of Rome, we yet join with them in this biblical regard for human life, including that of the unborn babe. (From the *Monthly Record*, the official organ of the Free Church of Scotland, in May, 1984.)

The Lambeth Conference of the Church of England is also on record as taking the same view:

> In the strongest terms Christians reject the practice of induced abortion, or infanticide, which involves the killing of a life already conceived (as well as a violation of the personality of the mother) save at the dictates of undeniable medical necessity . . . The sacredness of life is in Christian eyes an absolute which must not be violated. (Statement of the Lambeth Conference of Bishops, 1958.)

Despite all the assurances of pro-abortionists, there is massive evidence to show that the liberalisation of the laws on abortion in fact results in the cheapening of the view of human life, and also plays a major role in undermining the basis of the moral order upon which the foundations of modern civilisation rest.

Majority Christian opinion has always seen that where there is conflict between saving the life of the mother or the life of the child then it is always the mother who is saved. But when it comes to abortion – now almost on demand – for comfort, for convenience or to save social embarrassment we are moving in a totally different dimension.

Abortion at any stage (whether at the time the child breathes independently; at twenty-eight weeks; or earlier) eliminates a potential human being whose fellowship and love God could have enjoyed. Kagawa, the distinguished Japanese Christian who was responsible for introducing three-quarters of a million people to Christ, was labelled an illegitimate child of a Japanese dancing girl. The saintly Alexander Whyte of Scotland began life with a similar stigma. In fact there is no such thing as an illegitimate child – only illegitimate parents! But what a tragedy if they, and countless others like them, had never been given the opportunity and privilege of being born.

The other main medical issue is the practice of euthanasia. Its two principal forms are either withholding from the dying person that which would keep them alive or actually and positively deciding to inject death into a living body. Whichever of these two forms is adopted, it is difficult to see from the Bible how it is ever right to terminate a person's life when we have within our grasp the means of keeping them alive. It is true that we have discovered means of keeping people alive where fifty years ago they would certainly have died. These discoveries have laid heavier responsibilities upon those confronted by decisions which have life-and-death implications. Who is ever in a position to decide that another person's life has become intolerable? Who is ever in a position to conclude that the quality of a person's life is worse than death, and that that life may now legitimately be taken away? How is the word 'incurable' to be defined? At what stage of human suffering or human abnormality does a person become a fit subject for euthanasia?

Closely allied to the issue of euthanasia is the issue of suicide. Euthanasia does not appear in the Bible, but suicide does. Suicide is legally defined as, 'one who purposely destroys himself'. Suicide appears as an event in both Testaments, but there is no definite teaching about it. In the Old Testament there are at least five cases of a man taking his own life. Ahithophel took his own life after his counsel was rejected (2 Sam 17:23): Zimri, under seige, took his own life (1 Kgs 16:18); Abimilech, fearing the charge that he had been killed by a woman, ordered his armour-bearer to draw his sword and kill him when he had been fatally injured by a woman (Judg 9:24); Samson deliberately took his own life (Judg 16:23–31); and King Saul, conquered and wounded by the Philistines, fell upon his own sword (1 Sam 31:4, 5). In the New Testament Judas Iscariot flung the price of the betrayal of Jesus back at the priests and went and hanged himself (Matt 27:3–5).

We may well say that suicide always occurs when a man is in that moment of unsound mind. The fault in suicide appears to be two-fold. It involves running away from life and, as Thomas Aquinas saw, it usurps that which should belong to God alone for He alone has the right to bring life to an end. I have decided, after many years as a pastor and having been confronted by actual suicides through these years, that this is one place where condemnation should be silent, and where sympathy should be paramount. If there is ever a place where self-condemnation should emerge in a man's heart, it is here. The man who commits suicide does so because he finds life intolerable and it may be, and often it is, the case that that is so because no one could or would make it tolerable for him. It might well be true that there would be no suicides if there had been people to whom the person intent on suicide could have unburdened his mind and heart. How my own heart has grieved in all of these incidents of which I have been a part. I have concluded that when people are defeated by life I must leave them with trust to the mercy of God.

However, on the other hand, many under the severe pressure of life have sometimes felt that there was nowhere else for them to go and have contemplated taking their own lives and longed to die. In the Old Testament Elijah, David and Jeremiah all reached this low ebb. But they weathered the fierce storm, and in retrospect were thankful that neither they nor anyone else took the decision to end it all. They lived to realise that God had much more for them to do.

Both in euthanasia and in suicide the general effect is to lower the value of human life and the result of this is that more terrible things are liable to follow in any society. For this main reason, among many others, both euthanasia and suicide are to be resisted by society.

There are three attitudes which this Sixth Commandment recognises. Jesus, of course, took this commandment and transformed it. We have been wholly concerned with overt, physical, tangible killing. But Jesus is concerned not only with acts, but also with attitudes. He makes this abundantly clear in His Sermon on the Mount. He goes behind the act to the attitude which prompts it. The first attitude He deals with is *anger*. 'You have heard', He says, 'that people were told in the past, "Do not commit murder; anyone who does will be brought to trial." But now I tell you whoever is angry (without cause) with his brother will be brought to trial . . .' (Matt 5:21, 22). Here the Greek word is *orgizesthai*. In Greek there are two words for *anger*. One is *thumos* which is described as being like a flame which comes from dried straw. This is the anger which quickly blazes up and equally quickly dies down. The other is *orge* which describes an anger which has become inveterate. It is a long-lived anger. It is an anger which broods and the person will not allow it to die. It is this latter that Jesus condemns here.

The second attitude Jesus deals with is *arrogance*: '. . . whoever calls his brother "good-for-nothing" will be brought before the Council' (Matt 5:22). The word *raca* which is used here is an almost untranslatable word. It describes a tone of voice. Dr William Barclay speaks of *raca* as 'the word of one who despises another with an arrogant contempt'. The sin of inveterate anger is bad; the sin of contempt is just as bad. There is a kind of snobbery which murders human dignity and kills human personality. Sometimes it can be financial snobbery; sometimes social snobbery; sometimes intellectual snobbery. Snobbery may not be the lifting up of your hand against someone, but it is the lifting up of your mind and heart against them to dismiss them and destroy them.

The third attitude Jesus deals with is *abuse*: '... whoever calls his brother a worthless fool will be in danger of going to the fire of hell' (Matt 5:22). The word *moros* (from which we get our word moron) which is used here indicates a moral fool. It describes someone who is playing the fool in an immoral way. To call a man *moros* is not to criticise his mental ability, it is to condemn his moral character. It is to take his good name and reputation away from him. It is to brand him as a loose-living, immoral person.

Shakespeare's Iago says:

Who steals my purse steals trash; 'tis something, nothing;
'Twas mine, 'tis his, and has been slave to thousands;
But he who filches from me my good name
Robs me of that which naught enriches him,
And makes me poor indeed.

Jesus condemns this kind of character assassination.

The commandment which forbids murder has a relevance today as great as it had for the day and for the people to whom it was first given. Living the good life will require response to it not only negatively, but also positively in maintaining a peaceful heart, a humble spirit and a generous mind towards others. For the Christian, it is a commandment which refers not only to our actions, but also to our attitudes. Our relationships with people always begin in the heart and mind and not in the hands. Allow Christ to reign in your heart and mind, and your hands, as well as your lips, will always be under His control. Encouragement, rather than elimination will then be the dominating intention towards others in your life. This is an important part of the good life.

≈ 8 ≈

The Powder Keg

The first time I ever listened to a record of a sermon being preached – tapes were not yet in vogue – was to a sermon by Dr Peter Marshall. Peter Marshall had been born and raised in the neighbouring town to where I had been born and raised, and that gave a strange identity to the man who was now preaching from the pulpit of the historic old New York Avenue Presbyterian Church in Washington from where he had become Chaplain to the Senate of the United States of America. He had worked in the steel mills which dominated the part of Lanarkshire from which we came, and this following his running away to sea to join the Royal Navy at the age of fourteen. Peter Marshall's background, build and experience of life were all part of a robust personality which had to go to America to express itself fully. His wife Catherine, who was herself to become an outstanding contributor to Christian writing, says of him,

> 'So much did Dr Marshall love to preach, so sure was he that this was the thing God had designed him to do, that it was hard for him to turn down engagements. Though he had a rugged constitution – for Scotland's rigorous climate does not pamper – his strength did not quite equal his enthusiasm. On the morning of March 31, 1946, he collapsed in the pulpit with an attack of coronary thrombosis. After a few months convalescence, he launched into the most vigorous and productive period of his life.

> Then on January 25, 1949, at 8.15 in the morning, quietly he slipped through those phantom walls that separate this life from the next. We had only five hours' warning.'

Like all great preachers through the years, Peter Marshall said nothing new, but he said it in a new way. The huge congregations which regularly packed the church and overflowed into downstairs rooms were gripped anew by the gospel. It was this man who preached on sex in this way:

> The sex urge within each one of us is surely like a powder keg, useful, but dangerous . . .
>
> Next to hunger, the most powerful of human instincts is that of sex.
>
> You cannot escape from it, for you are made that way. It pulses in your blood, sings in your throat and shines in your eyes.
>
> Now, sex will be either the nicest thing in your life – or it will be the nastiest – depending on whether you use it or abuse it. Only in nasty minds are there nasty thoughts about sex.
>
> There is nothing shameful about the sex urge, but some people let it urge them to do shameful things . . .

It is with this powder keg, 'useful, but dangerous', that the Seventh Commandment is concerned. According to the Bible, sex is part of the human scene for two reasons. Obviously, it exists for the procreation of the human species, but first of all it has been made part of our humanity to secure and strengthen the bonding partnership of marriage. To lose a biblical perspective of sex is to loosen seriously the unique relationship of marriage significantly. To do this is to plot the course for the decline of a society and civilisation. There have been eighty-eight civilisations which have risen, plateaued, declined, and ultimately fallen. This procedure has been carefully studied and the same pattern for a civilisation's decline and fall emerges in all cases without exception. During the rise of a civilisation family life has been strong and stable and heterosexual marriage is regarded as permanent. During the decline of a civilisation family life disintegrates, divorce is common and accepted, and sexual permissiveness is regarded as the norm. As we move towards the end of the twentieth century in Britain, quite clearly the family is under serious threat. The family is central to the social, economic and moral well-being of our nation and yet both government and citizen exert little strength to sustain it. The current Aids campaign to combat a disease which will kill the equivalent of a jumbo-jet load of Britons every month at its present rate of development, gives a sharp insight into the values allowed to survive at Whitehall – our seat of government. At present the chief consideration which seems to motivate our legislators is fear of offending the 'gay community'. Such terms as chastity outside of marriage and fidelity within marriage are shamefacedly avoided and the defeatist assumption is endorsed that sexual licence is now general and irreversible.

The legally defined monogamous family unit has always been a civilising element in society. But in the twentieth century it has acquired poignant significance as a protective force for the threatened individual against the ravages of the state. It has become an area of private custom as opposed to public law. It upholds non-material values and makes them paramount. It scorns the exclusive economics of profit-and-loss. It rejects political ideology as the sole guide to life. The family is, in fact, a gentle, natural set of beliefs in itself, a system of morality based on altruism. It embraces tradition rather than fashionable dogma. It upholds a fair balance of rights and responsibilities, and not merely within one generation. It insists on respect for the past and concern for the future. We are to farm, not plunder, the earth, honour the memory and heed the wishes of our forebears, plan not just for ourselves but for posterity – all this is family doctrine and the Seventh Commandment stands sentinel over it.

An increasing number of borough councils in the United Kingdom, in their education policy, are encouraging children to regard homosexuality as acceptable, and they provide financial and institutional aid to this end. Increasingly, marriage and the family are treated as merely one of the various 'life-styles' or 'orientations' and all other expressions of human sexuality are equally legitimate. Significantly the foot-soldiers of every inner city riot are those who have never known a proper home.

It is no accident that the totalitarian regimes of our times have sought to replace family ties by state-ideological ones. Mussolini of Italy declared: 'Everything FOR the state, nothing AGAINST the state. Nothing OUTSIDE the state'. Power was to be built on the smoking ruins of family love. Stalin of Russia included members of his own family among his myriad victims. Mussolini murdered his own son-in-law. One of the Hitler's last acts was to murder his mistress's brother. Goebbels, one of Hitler's senior colleagues, massacred his own children. Hitler's female SS storm-troopers toured the concentration camps to kidnap infants for the race farms.

In Russia retaliation against the family remains the most effective weapon of the KGB, widely imitated in the petty horror-states of some Afro-Asian nations.

Conversely, in all the successful efforts to re-create humane societies in the post-war era, stress on the family has been a potent element. Konrad Adenauer, himself the patriarch of a vast family, came to regard it as the one dependable refuge from totalitarian invasion. It was on the basis of the family, closely associated with individualism and voluntarism, that he set about his great work of rebuilding Germany after the Hitlerian catastrophe.

De Gasperi in Italy and de Gaulle in France likewise used the family as the focus and instrument of natural regeneration. In Japan, the post-war reforms inspired a new individualism by encouraging the emergence, as an alternative centre of loyalty to the state, of the family and the many Japanese institutions which embody the family image. Japanese firms, modelled on the family and providing the same sense of belonging, have been at the heart of its economic miracle.

The family principle, as opposed to state collectivism, underlies the success of all the enterprise economics of East Asia, in Korea and Taiwan, in Singapore and Hong Kong, as well as in Japan. Wherever in the post-war world the family has been honoured, cultivated and reinforced, instead of invaded and undermined, prosperity has normally followed.

What a tragedy it has been in our time that the Department of Health officials fought a long campaign, crowned with victory by the Law Lords, to allow National Health Service doctors to provide under-age girls with contraceptive advice without the knowledge and against the wishes of their parents. It is hard to conceive of a more damaging assault on the whole concept of the family and parental responsibility.

It was with shrewd insight that Mr Justice Denning, afterwards to become the Master of the Rolls, in May 1954 said: 'We have reached a position unfortunately, I fear, where adultery – or infidelity or misconduct as soft-hearted people call it – is considered to be a matter of little moment. It is no bar to advancement to any offices of State, high or low, whereas any other form of stealing would mean the end of a career'. The whole climate of our society would warmly endorse the view that it is much better for two people who are in love, but are not married, to live together than it is for two people who are not in love, but are married, to live together. By and large the climate in our society affirms that it can hardly be wrong for people to follow their inclinations. If the first marriage they contracted into was a mistake, possibly entered into too hastily, then why must a couple live together in misery when all the time happiness is waiting for them just round the corner in the person of some other man or woman? Surely it is better to cut your losses and begin all over again? The chances of making the same mistake twice are greatly reduced, and there are thousands of happy marriages which have emerged from this kind of chaos. Such is the plausible argument which runs in one form or another through our society. Adultery is not considered too wrong so long as it doesn't hurt anyone and provided there is true love behind it. A and B are married. B meets C when things are not going too well with A. The consequence is that C meets D because things have deteriorated with B. So you can get a number of interesting equations, the most common of which is (A + D) and (B + C) = three wrecked marriages + three broken homes + four damaged people. Variations on this theme form the subject matter of some of our most popular films, novels and plays.

Why does God lay down the rule in the Bible that sexual intercourse between two people, either of whom is married to someone else, is wrong? Is it simply that God watches things which seem to give pleasure and happiness to people and steps in, in an arbitrary way, and stops it? Is it that God is the world's master kill-joy? Many have concluded that this is so – God is capricious and frustrates man's natural and God-given instincts. It is not only in Exodus 20:14 that this prohibition is cited, but also in Leviticus 18:20; Deuteronomy 5:18; Jeremiah 5:7, 8; 7:9; 23:11; 29:23 and so on. What is so wrong with adultery? Is it because it is physical and sexual? These two areas of our humanity cause a great deal of awkwardness and embarrassment to many Christians at least. Background, environment and faulty teaching have all contributed to grave suspicion over anything to do with our humanity and our sexuality. But God created us in this way so He could never condemn the reality that He created. The Bible speaks of adultery as ungodly. Is it because God does not have a body and so sexuality is not His experience? That cannot be so either, since man has been created 'in the image of God' and 'male and female created He them'. In other words there is something in the sexual relationship between men and women which mirrors some significant reality in the nature of God. Man has been created to be like God and so he has to live his life as 'a chip off the old block'.

Fundamentally, adultery is disloyalty. It is this which is so unlike God. Men and women created to manifest the reality of God, who are involved in adultery, demonstrate disloyalty – and this is a deep distortion of the nature of God. God's love is loyal. When God falls in love, He stays in love. It is said of His only Son Jesus Christ, who came not only to redeem mankind, but also to reveal God to mankind, that 'having loved His own He loved them to the very end' despite their imperfections and failures. The most frequent phrase on the lips of God towards His people is 'I will'. The Hebrew word which is used for God's love is *heseth* – 'covenant love' or 'loyalty'. We carry this over into the Christian marriage ceremony. We require people who are married in church not simply to affirm that they will love each other, but solemnly vow that they will be loyal to each other 'for better, for worse; for richer for poorer; in sickness and in health; to love and to cherish until they shall be separated by death'. To that awesome, far-reaching, demanding loyalty they declare 'I will'. On this foundation adultery can never stand. There are other significant reasons, however, which make adultery wrong and destructive. To see these reasons is to go a long way to build a firm rock against the flood-tide of our society which has, by and large, submitted to a conclusion that adultery is inevitable and so acceptable.

First of all we need to see the distinctiveness of sex in the human personality. After the instinct of hunger our sexual impulse is the strongest instinct in our human make-up. Universally, it is bound up with the totality of life. It cannot be compartmentalised. Society in general, and the humanist in particular, would argue that sex is no different from any other physical appetite. There are desires inherent in our bodies which demand to be satisfied. We need food because our bodies cry out in hunger; we need drink because our bodies cry out in thirst; we need sleep because our bodies cry out in weariness – and sex comes into this same category. We are basically, at a physical level, animal in our instincts and these have to be satisfied otherwise serious problems arise.

To include sex in this category is to conclude that there is no moral difference between preferring the wife next door's steak-and-kidney pie to preferring the wife next door to our own. Something instinctively tells us that there is a difference. What is that difference? During the course of history the human race has tried every conceivable arrangement for the man/woman relationship because of the fundamental sex drive – promiscuity; free love; prostitution; trial marriage; polygamy, etc; and always these have been unsatisfactory, not only for the individual, but also for society. God's way has always been monogamy (one man and one woman relating exclusively to each other). Some may question this in view of the relationships entered into by some of the Old Testament saints. Some of them were polygamous! However, the Bible records life with honesty and tells the story like it is with stubborn and complete honesty. In recording polygamous relationships the Bible never once indicates that these relationships were ever entered into under the direction of God. These are not God's way!

Clearly the Bible indicates that sex involves the whole of our personality and not just a part. Sex is not just a physical thing, but a personality thing. Writing to the erring Christians in Corinth Paul says, 'Avoid immorality [literally: "flee sexual impurity"]. Any other sin a man commits does not affect his body as this one does; but the man who is guilty of sexual immorality sins against his own body' (1 Cor 6:18). Sexual immorality has a much more far reaching effect in our living than hunger, thirst or tiredness. In the Bible 'the body' includes the psychological aspect of our nature as well as the physical aspect. Eating someone else's pie does not involve the whole personality whereas sex does. In giving yourself to someone sexually you give yourself not simply physically, but psychologically and emotionally. You are, in other words, involved as a person and not just as a stomach. The wise writer of the Book of Proverbs (6:32) says in a pretty comprehensive and devastating way, 'But a man who commits adultery doesn't have any sense. He is just destroying himself'.

Not only does sex affect our whole personality in a general sense, but it has a spiritual aspect to it in a particular sense. I am very concerned not to fall into a very destructive trap here. Over the years Christians have often adopted extreme attitudes towards sex in a spiritual context. They have either denigrated sex and declared, or implied, that it is dirty or else they have elevated it and put it on a high spiritual, mystical plane. Both conclusions are wrong. God neither denigrates nor elevates sex, but indicates it is something to be expressed, experienced and enjoyed within the security and responsibility of the marriage relationship. However, there is something in the marriage relationship which corresponds to something which is deeply spiritual. How else can the Song of Songs be understood in the Old Testament. Christians have found in that song expressions they want to use in their relationship to the Lord. In the New Testament (particularly in Eph 5:21–33) marriage is taught as intended to mirror the relationship between Christ and the Church.

In all of this there is a basic and unmistakable principle which emerges that to regard sex simply as a physical thing and to treat it simply as an appetite, is to misunderstand it, and consequently to spoil it.

The *second* thing which we need to do is to define marriage. The world tacitly defines marriage as a relationship of convenience. If she washes and irons my clothes, then I will dig and cultivate the garden. If she cooks my food then I will provide the housekeeping money. If she cleans the house and runs its daily affairs then I will take care of the car and the holiday in the summer. If she cooperates sexually then I will cooperate socially. In other words it is better for us to combine forces rather than keep moving from your house to my house, and from my house to your house. After all don't they say that 'Two can live as cheaply as one'? Marriage is a convenient way for two people to care for the needs of the other. The implication, however, is equally clear that when she no longer launders my clothes; cooks my food; and attends to my house, then I no longer have a responsibility to cultivate the garden;

provide the mortgage; or arrange the summer holiday. The division of labour and responsibility is no longer being adhered to so the reason for being together is no longer valid. Many marriages exist and disappear on this basis – the basis of convenience.

Much more overtly – especially when it is dealt with in legal terms – marriage is seen as a contract that two people more or less willingly and voluntarily enter into. Two people agree to do certain things for each other and with each other as long as they want to – but the time may come when they feel that they have had enough and so quite clinically and coldly the contract can be cancelled. It becomes rather like a job where I can offer my energy and expertise to an employer who will enter into a contract with me to pay for what I am offering and agree certain conditions. That contract can be set aside with notice given by either side of one month or three months or whatever the contract says. So in marriage it is now possible to cancel the contract under certain conditions in as short a time as one year – Lord Hailsham's Matrimonial and Family Proceedings Bill makes it possible for the marriage to be dissolved within a year providing both parties consent. It is estimated that this Bill will affect 170,000 couples in the UK each year.

Socially, a number of trends are observable. For example 1977 was the first year when there were more marriages in the registrar's office than in church. So traditional Christian values for marriage were being set aside. Again, more and more people are not getting married at all. Why bother with a piece of paper and a ceremony and a reception? We love each other; isn't that enough? We want to live together now so why shouldn't we? And incidentally the tax laws are weighted in our favour if we remain single! There are other alternatives which offer their own appeal – communal marriages or wife swapping; homosexual marriages (not yet here in the United Kingdom, but already practised in some parts of the United States); cohabitation (within the last ten years the number of couples who live together before marriage has tripled according to the government's general household survey). In a study covering 21,000 people in 12,500 households it was shown that 66 per cent of the women under 35 years who married in the early eighties had been co-habiting with their husbands. In the early seventies the proportion was 13 per cent. The average time which couples lived together before marriage was over twelve months for first-time couples and over two years for second marriages.

Those who accept what the Bible says about marriage are a small minority in this country. The Bible says that marriage is not a matter of convenience or contract or social custom, but a commitment. Each marriage is the inauguration of something never before seen in the world. Hugh Robert MacDonald defines it,

> Christian marriage is a gift of God: it is a new relationship of love which God gives to those who love and obey Him; it is the joining of two destinies, the fusion of two personalities in such a glorious way that a man and a woman cease to be separate individuals and are caught up together in a new communion with God. As a violin and a bow are one; as a lock and a key are one, so a husband and his wife, when united by God in Christian marriage, are one.

I realise that there are some good marriages experienced without Christian faith being a living part of them, but this is God's best.

The Bible says that two become one – not just in a sexual act, but one person. If two become one then each has become a half of a completed new whole. The married person is only half a person now. As long as the other partner remains alive they remain that. One is incomplete without the other. This is the biblical insight into marriage. Marriage is the breaking of one relationship – with the parents – and the making of a completely new relationship – with the partner.

When Jesus was asked about divorce, He answered in terms

of Genesis 2. When divorce is asked for you are not separating two people, you are in fact dividing one person. You are dismembering one body, for biblically one plus one equals one. This is why divorce is so devastatingly painful and destructive. It is not a question of two people who decided to live together now living separately. It is two people who have become one tearing that single unit in halves. This is the heart of Jesus' teaching on divorce. To re-marry a divorced person is to marry half a person.

In the Bible there is only one thing which restores wholeness to a half person, and that is death. According to Mark 12 and Romans 7 on earth half-ness will be restored to wholeness at death.

The *third* thing we need to do is to acknowledge that sentiment or feelings are a very insecure base for permanence in marriage. There are three views of the kind of love which will establish a firm basis for marriage.

1. The *romantic* view of love – this emphasises the emotions
2. The *rational* view of love – this emphasises the mind
3. The *religious* view of love – this emphasises the will.

We need to explore all three since love has become a debased word and a great deal of confusion occupies many intelligent minds.

1. Romantic love

Here love is defined in terms of how I feel about a person. Love starts when I have romantic feelings about someone, but stops when these romantic feelings disappear. 'Love is a feeling you feel when you feel that you are going to feel a feeling that you have never felt before'. The implication of this is that love is something over which you have absolutely no control. We encapsulate this by talking about 'falling in love'. This is the majority view today. It is a concept which has swept through the Western world and has been encouraged by both the large and the small screens. A well-known marriage and family counsellor has given a very powerful description of a marriage based on romantic love.

> The confusion begins when boy meets girl and the entire sky lights up in romantic profusion. Smoke and fire are followed by lightning and thunder, and also two trembly-voiced adolescents find themselves knee-deep in true love. Adrenalin, and 64 other hormones, are dumped into the cardio-vascular system by the pint and every nerve is charged with electricity. Then two little fellows go racing up the respective back-bones and blast their exhilarating message into each spinning head: 'This is it! The search is over! You have found the perfect human being! Hurray for love!'
>
> For our romantic young couple it is simply too wonderful to behold. They want to be together twenty-four hours a day, to take walks in the rain; to sit by the fire; and kiss and munch and cuddle. They get all choked up just thinking about each other and it doesn't take long for the subject of marriage to arise. So they set the date; reserve the church; and contact the minister; and order the flowers. The big day arrives amidst mother's tears, and dad's grins, and jealous bridesmaids, and bratty little flower-girls. The candles are lit, and two beautiful songs are butchered by the bride's sister. Then the vows are muttered and the rings are placed on trembling fingers and the minister tells the groom to kiss his new wife.
>
> Then they sprint up the aisle—each flashing thirty-two teeth on the way to the reception. Their friends and well-wishers hug and kiss the bride and roll their eyes at the groom and eat the awful cake and follow the instructions of the perspiring photographer. Finally the new Mr and Mrs run from the church in a flurry of confetti and strike out for their honeymoon. So far the beautiful dream remains intact. But it is living on borrowed time.
>
> The first night in the hotel is not only less exciting than advertised, it turns into a comical disaster. About 3 o'clock

on the second afternoon he gives ten minutes serious thought to the fateful question: 'Have I made an enormous mistake?' His silence increases her anxiety and the seeds of disenchantment are sown. Each partner has far too much time to think about the consequences of this new relationship and they both begin to feel trapped.

Their initial argument is a silly thing – they struggle over how much money to spend for dinner on the third night of their honeymoon. She wants to go to somewhere romantic to charge up the atmosphere and he wants to eat at Wimpey's. The flare up only lasts a few minutes and is followed by apologies. But some harsh words have been exchanged which took the keen edge off the beautiful dream. They will soon learn to hurt each other much more effectively. Somehow they make it through the six-day trip, and drive home to set up house together.

Then the world starts to splinter and disintegrate before their eyes. The next fight is bigger and better than the first. He leaves home for two hours and she calls her mother. Throughout the first year they will both be engaged in an enormous contest of wills, each vying for power and leadership, and in the midst of this tug-of-war she staggers out of the obstetrician's office with the words ringing in her ears: 'I have some good news for you, Mrs Jones!' If there is anything in the world that Mrs Jones doesn't need at that moment it is good news from the obstetrician.

From there to the final conflict we see two disappointed, confused and deeply hurt young people wondering how it all came about. We also see a little lad who will never enjoy the benefits of a stable home. He will be raised by his mother, and will always wonder, 'Why doesn't dad live here anymore?'

All of this began because that marriage was at the mercy of something over which neither had any control – their feelings. Obviously this is a highly unsatisfactory view of love regarding a permanent relationship.

2. *Rational love*

Now we transfer the view of love from the heart to the head. This view is no longer common – or even acceptable within our culture. The marriage partnership is analysed, appraised, sifted and weighed. The pros and cons are balanced out for the couple according to temperament, environment, social standing, physical stature and health, religious conviction, political viewpoint, and so on.

There is a story told of two people – I think, perhaps, apocryphal – where the man says to the woman, 'I'm making a list of your good points and when I get to twenty, I will ask you to marry me. I have got to fifteen'. To this she replies, 'You had better hurry up, because I am making a list of your bad points and when I get to twenty I will not even consider marrying you. I have got to nineteen'. It does illustrate however – whether true or fanciful – love seen in terms of the operation of the mind.

In view of the strong antipathy within Western culture to this attitude and activity in determining a marriage partnership, it needs to be said that we must be careful not to be too sweeping in ruling out of court the place of the mind in approaching a relationship.

3. *Religious love*

In defining love which will be a fitting base for a permanent relationship, the heart and the head – though important and playing their part – are not considered sufficient. The heart of love rests not on how you feel, or on what you think and know, but on the way you act and the attitude you have towards the one so loved. By far the commonest New Testament word for love is the noun *agape* and the verb *agapan.* It would not be true to say that the New Testament never used anything else but *agape* and *agapan* to express Christian love. *Philein* is sometimes used. It is used in the Gospel of John (5:20) for the Father's love for the Son; and of God's love for men (16:27). It is used by Paul of the devotion men ought to bear towards Jesus (1 Cor 16:22). Although *philein* has a lovely warmth about it and means to look on someone with affectionate regard, and can be used for the love of friendship and for the love of husband and of wife, it can best be translated 'to cherish'. However the occurrences of *philein* in the New Testament are comparatively few, while *agape* occurs almost 120 times and *agapan* more than 130 times. *Agape* has to do with mind: it is not simply an emotion which rises unbidden in our hearts; it is a principle by which we deliberately live. *Agape* has supremely to do with the will. It is a conquest, a victory, an achievement. It is in fact the power to love the unlovable, to love people we do not like. Christianity does not ask us to love our enemies and to love men and women at large in the same way as we love our nearest and dearest and those who are closest to us; that would be at one and the same time impossible and wrong. But it does demand that we should have at all times a certain attitude of the mind and a certain direction of the will towards all men, no matter who they are whether marriage partner or otherwise. *Agape* is the spirit which says, 'No matter what you do to me, I will never seek to do harm to you; I will never set out for revenge; I will always seek nothing but your highest good'. Christian love is unconquerable benevolence and invincible goodwill. Such love is not possible without the Christian dynamic – the real ministry of the Holy Spirit.

The love which is within true marriage of course must contain romantic feeling and rational understanding, but when a couple stand before me to be married (having already spent several hours in pre-marriage counselling) I do not ask them what their feelings are for each other at that moment nor do I ask if they consider themselves to be well-matched or if their parents approve of the relationship. Nor do they reply that they feel or think they love the one standing beside them. I ask them if they will be loyal to each other in strength or in weakness, through laughter and tears, whether they succeed or fail.

This is true love in God's sight because it is the love which God has for us. It is a love which is not conditioned by what He either feels or thinks about us. It is the kind of love which categorically and resolutely says, 'I will'. If this is so then love does not cease when I no longer feel as I used to or as I have sometimes felt. If this is so then love does not cease when I can produce pretty well every reason and argument for breaking up marriage.

This Commandment protects that kind of love – it is supernatural love; Holy Spirit love; Calvary love. It is the kind of love that God wants all men and women to experience and express. It is the kind of love which makes adultery not only unacceptable, but unthinkable.

The *fourth* thing we need to do is to see the danger of separation. It is true that separation is counselled in the Bible, 'However, if the one who is not a believer wishes to leave the Christian partner, let it be so. In such cases the Christian partner, whether husband or wife, is free to act' (1 Cor 7:15). It needs to be noted that this statement is made within the context of pastoral counselling and not divine commandment. This situation relates to those who have become Christians after marriage. For the sake of peace in the home the unbelieving partner may wish to leave and so is to be allowed to go. The Bible clearly teaches that Christians should not marry non-Christians. More and more frequently today, however, one partner becomes a Christian after the marriage has begun. This can, and often does, lead to tension which the non-Christian partner cannot and will not tolerate. So far as the Christian partner is concerned he/she is to maintain the relationship with humility, grace, patience and beauty by the supernatural resources which God makes available by the Holy Spirit – this is *agape*.

Separation, however, not infrequently leads to divorce and divorce leads to re-marriage within our society. God clearly and categorically hates divorce (Mal 2:16). Jesus surely reflected the Father's attitude. Divorce is alien to God's plan for His people. It is very easy to be swept along by how we feel and by how society thinks, but separation and re-marriage are two separate things. The Bible makes the heart of God painfully clear to us: 'For married people I have a command which is not my own but the Lord's: a wife must not leave her husband; but if she does she must remain single or else be reconciled to her husband; and a husband must not divorce his wife'.

Even in the celebrated 'exception clause' of Matthew 19:9 there is serious controversy over the word *porneia*, which is translated unchastity or fornication. There are good linguistic grounds for concluding that Jesus is not referring here to something which happens after marriage has been entered into, but something which happened prior to the marriage taking place, and had not been disclosed. This would affirm a very narrow and specialised exception. Others, however, would take a wider view of *porneia* and conclude that it is not referring to unchastity prior to marriage, but to infidelity sexually within the marriage. However it is understood the central issue remains that God has a strong antipathy to divorce and a clear demand for permanence in the marriage relationship.

Most of what has already been said in this chapter is intensely personal. However, this whole area has wider, social implications. As a brick to a building, so marriage is to a society. If you take enough bricks out of a building it will very quickly become unstable. If you continue this process the building will ultimately collapse. So it is with marriage and society – the more marriages that crumble and fail, the more unstable and frail a society becomes. To allow this process to continue is to hasten the complete disintegration of a society. Professor E. O. James, writing in *Marriage and Society* (1952) says, '. . . by bringing discord into the domestic group and making family life insecure it has a harmful effect on society. Therefore in all states of culture, restrictions, often in the form of stringent taboos, have been enforced to prevent any irregularities which would prove to be socially disturbing and injurious.' Historically this is certainly true. We are examining here not simply a personal issue, but a serious social one. Unhappily the fabric of society does not always command a significant place in personal responsibility – even among Christians!

In all of this it is necessary for us to return to the basics which God indicates for true fulfilment in marriage. *First* of all it is not too difficult to see and understand that the real difficulty in any marriage is not sexual incompatibility or financial pressure or any other single factor. The real difficulty in any marriage is human nature. This is the basic problem behind broken homes. C. S. Lewis once said, 'No clever arrangement of bad eggs ever made a good omelette'. Just so! What is needed is not readjustment or reformation within the marriage, but regeneration in the hearts of both partners. Hartley Coleridge, in his poem *Regeneration*, sets down the need and longing of the human heart simply and helpfully:

> I want a cleansing change within,
> My life must once again begin;
> New hope I need and youth renewed,
> And more than human fortitude;
> New faith, new love, and strength to cast
> Away the fetters of the past.

I cannot say how this happens. Jesus Himself describes it as a mystery and a mystery it remains. But if I do not know how it happens, I certainly know that it can and does happen. Henry Drummond once said, 'There is nothing more unintelligible in the world than how a soul is born again. There is nothing more intelligible than that it is! We can understand the fact, however, without necessarily understanding the act'. The apostle Paul writing a letter to the Christians at Corinth who had their own spiritual, moral, and social problems said, 'When someone becomes a Christian he becomes a brand new person inside. He is not the same any more. A new life has begun. All these new things are from God who brought us back to himself through what Christ Jesus did'. This is a fact which I have seen again and again over the years transforming not only marriages, but many other situations besides. I remember attending one of our evening services. I was not taking part at the front that night and the only place I could find a seat was in the gallery of the church. I sat near to the end of the seat and as the service was beginning a young woman came in and squeezed into the small space that remained at the very end of the seat. I did not know her and the service had begun. I was aware at one point in the service that she was weeping. As the service closed I turned to greet her. She said to me, 'You do not know who I am, but I am Roger's wife!' Now Roger had become a Christian not too long before and the vitality and radiance of his faith was transparent. I had already been so encouraged on so many occasions by it. Because of deep and serious problems which he had had his marriage had foundered and eventually fallen apart. Separation and divorce followed. I knew that this troubled him deeply. Now I was sitting beside his divorced wife, Anne. She told me that night that on the previous Sunday evening she had become a Christian in the evening service. I was sitting beside someone who was one week old spiritually. I was thrilled, excited, filled with wonder. Much later on that evening I began to wonder what would happen now. The weeks and the months passed. There were hurts and wounds to heal. There was a great deal of ground to cover, but with patience, humility and good humour Roger and Anne began to cover that ground. It was far from easy, and all kinds of doubts and insecurities began to emerge, but as the months passed these two forthright, stubbornly honest Christians worked things through. The day came when I married them for the second time – to each other.

During the early part of their wedding I asked two questions of each of them. First of all I asked:

> Do you confess your past failure and before God repent of it and receive the forgiveness and cleansing of God?

Both in turn replied: 'I do'.
Then I asked:

> As we now close the door on the past and declare under God that you are now free from it, do you intend, with God's help, to live in the freedom with which Jesus has set you free?

Both in turn replied: 'I do'.
I went on to say:

> Our Lord Jesus Christ through His death on the Cross and by His resurrection from the dead has freed us not only from the guilt of sin, but also from its power over us, so that by the indwelling of the Holy Spirit we should live in righteousness and peace.
>
> May He this day pardon and deliver you from all your sins, and confirm and strengthen you in all goodness, and keep you in eternal life, through Jesus Christ our Lord.

So we closed the door on the past securely so that when difficult days come in the future the enemy will have no power or opportunity to accuse or condemn. So a deeply moving wedding service continued and marked a new beginning for Roger and Anne.

Not only is regeneration by the Spirit of God necessary for a marriage to follow God's prescription, but *secondly* both partners need to recognise the significance of love. Love needs to be seen to be in the area of the will rather than in the area of the emotion. Love needs to exercise our will much more strongly than our feelings. When a bride and bridegroom truly understand the nature of the vows they take to each other on their wedding day they are saying by implication very directly:

> My love for you will not depend on time or circumstance or feeling. Whatever you turn out to be, whether you bring me a blessing or a curse, whether you help me or hinder me, whether you give me happiness or break my heart, I will remain forever true to you. My love will be as faithful as God's love. I put my life in your hands.

A relationship based on this kind of love may well undergo serious assault and heavy pressure. It may well shake and be on the point of collapse. But it will not fail, and it must endure. It will survive where others have perished, not because these partners were paragons of virtue, but because they understood the nature of the relationship they were entering, the impossibility of maintaining it by human endeavour and the necessity of looking for and finding divine enabling through the Holy Spirit.

Finally God always intended that in marriage we would respond to the desires of His Son Jesus Christ. Saint Exupery in *Wind, Sand and Stars* says, 'Life has taught us that love doesn't consist in gazing at each other, but in looking outward together in the same direction'. When that direction is Christ, then hope must inevitably dawn. Recently I married a couple whom I had been instructing in marriage over the past year. The week before their wedding they brought vows to me which they asked me to confirm and check. With one small omission, I can share these with you as they resulted from our talks together on Christian marriage.

> I, A, take you, B, to be my wife, to have and to hold, from this day forward. I commit myself to you for better for worse, for richer for poorer, in sickness and in health, to love and to cherish. And I commit myself to helping you to grow in accordance with God's will for you, and where I feel unable to do this in my own strength, I promise to go to God in prayer and seek the enabling power of His Spirit, until death us do part, according to God's holy law; and this is my solemn vow.'

She took a similar vow with one addition 'to obey' as well as 'to love and cherish'.

I do not know what lies ahead for them, but I anticipate an enriching and fruitful marriage.

How is it possible to respond to this Seventh Commandment when the temptation to break it is strong? In that hour the nature of the commitment to loyalty which has been made will need to be recalled and affirmed if integrity is to be maintained. The reality of Christ dwelling in our hearts by His Spirit will need to be realised and exposed. If a spark falls on the pavement nothing happens. When a spark falls on a petrol tank there is an explosion. The temptation to commit adultery falls on the man who recalls his commitment and recognises the Lordship of Christ like a spark falling on water or concrete; but when the spark of temptation falls on the heart of a man who ignores his commitment and disregards his Lord, it is like a spark falling on a powder keg and the living bomb explodes!

≈ 9 ≈

Safeguard Man's and God's Possessions

It is no sin to have things. It is sinful to be greedy and to exploit others in order to have them. It is no sin to enjoy what we have. It is sinful to be exclusive and selfish in the way that we possess what we have. There are those who have concluded that Christianity undergirds the political philosophy of Communism. Nothing could be further from the truth. Communism is the state violation of the Eighth Commandment. Christian fellowship – which involves not only sharing possessions, but sharing lives – and Marxist Communism are poles apart, though Karl Marx, like Jesus, was a Jew who got his convictions and principles from the Old Testament prophets. There is a key passage in the Acts of the Apostles (4:32–35) where Christian fellowship is seen to be operating not only with social effectiveness, but also with spiritual dynamism. However, there are significant differences between what is recorded there and political Communism as we know it today. These men and women in Acts were one 'in mind and heart' – nobody had to force anyone else to do or accept anything. The reason for sharing what they had was the result of love motivating from within rather than law imposing from without.

Secondly, they were all baptised in the Holy Spirit. There was a deeply spiritual base for what they were experiencing and expressing. They were united in spirit as well as in mind, emotion and will. Communism is avowedly atheistic and proclaims religious reality as a significant hindrance to social health and well-being.

Thirdly, what was happening was spontaneous – no one told them what to do. The events occurring within that infant church in Jerusalem were not simply a good idea which had to be organised. They were not asking questions like, 'Do we have to do this?' or 'Must we do this?' They were looking for practical opportunities to express their spiritual reality.

Fourthly, their property was not being taken from them. It was entirely in their control to do with as they wished (Acts 5:4). Their property was in the hands of neither the State nor the Church. What is happening here is not the abolition of private property in principle, but the sharing of it in practice.

Fifthly, they were achieving something which a Communist state has never achieved. The Communist aim is to take from each according to his ability and give to each according to his need, but the communist reality is that from each is taken according to his ability, but to each is given according to his work. So far, in history, it is only where the Christian dynamic is functioning that ability and need can be brought together with no strings attached.

Sixthly, Communism is based on hatred of the rich, whereas Christianity is based on love and commitment to the poor.

Finally, Christianity is concerned to express itself locally, whereas Communism is concerned to exercise its convictions universally. So however it appears, and whatever is said, Christianity and Communism are fundamentally different.

When it comes to possessions there are five attitudes which we have noticed within our own church. There are those who turn up from time to time and either attempt to integrate with us or sometimes do not even bother to do that, and soon it becomes clear what they have come for. In a variety of ways they will express themselves, but when all is said and done they have concluded that we have an obligation to share with them whatever we have. They demonstrate a blackmailing attitude which implies, 'since you are Christians what you have is to be given to me'. That can never be true since privilege will always involve responsibility and accountability. Secondly, there are those among us who either overtly or tacitly have concluded that 'what is mine is my own'. We have earned it, saved it, worked for it, inherited it – it is mine. That attitude cannot be defended either. Thirdly, there is an attitude which says: 'what is mine is yours'. For some years I believed that this was the Christian way, since it involves a voluntary use of possessions, and taught the congregation that it was so. Then one of our elders got alongside me and encouraged me to see a fourth reality that 'what is mine is ours'. That certainly brought me into a new depth and understanding of Christian fellowship.

However, I have concluded that the highest way of all for regarding and handling our possessions is to come to the place where I am totally convinced that 'what I have is His'. If this is really so then my whole attitude to what I have and how I use what I have is completely transformed. I have seen this attitude worked out in practical terms by some within our own congregation. It can operate powerfully whether the person who endorses it is rich or poor. It is expressed by a lady called Mrs Beswick who lived in East London during the dark, traumatic days of the blitz of World War II. She had been an officer in the Salvation Army, but had grown old and had had to be released from active service. She had little, but gave so much. Concerned that even her little belonged to Christ, and so should be available, she put a large card in her window: 'If you need help, knock here'. In the same way Lord Justice Cairns at the turn of the century was talking to a workman and he said:

> If you came to my house, you'd probably think it luxurious. You'd say that with all this I should be a happy man. I am – but my furniture and food have nothing to do with it. Every day I rise with the consciousness that God loves me and cares for me. He has forgiven all my sins for Christ's

sake. And I look forward to the future with no dread. If I could be convinced that this is a delusion, my home would give me little repose, and my food would often be untasted. It is a joy to me to tell you that the costly things in my home, which you cannot share with me, are not the things of which my happiness is made. Else I should wonder why they are given to so few. If tomorrow I left my house for a hovel I would take my joy with me. It is Christ alone who satisfies.

Both Mrs Beswick and Lord Justice Cairns demonstrate a right attitude to what they possess. God's concern is basically about how we get what we possess and then how we use it.

The Sixth Commandment is about the sanctity of life. The Seventh Commandment is about the sanctity of marriage. This Eighth Commandment is about the sanctity of property. This commandment is absolute and offers no qualifications and is repeated frequently in the Bible. It is quoted in Leviticus 19:11 and in Deuteronomy 5:19. When the prophets rebuke the sins and the disobedience of Israel, theft and stealing again and again come under their condemnation. The curse is on him who steals, and he will be cut off (Zech 5:3). If the wicked wishes to live, the first thing he must do is to restore what he has stolen (Ezek 33:15). The condemnation is that the people of this land have practised extortion and committed robbery (Ezek 22:29). Amos condemns those who store up violence and robbery (Amos 3:10). Isaiah speaks of the princes who are the companions of thieves (Isa 1:23). Prophet and lawgiver alike show the prevalence of stealing and the horror of it. In fact the law of the Old Testament does not simply condemn stealing; it has a great deal to say about the penalty for it. The spectrum of punishment spans from significant restitution to capital punishment.

Society, however, would want to submit quite a number of qualifications to this absolute commandment which is so simply and straightforwardly given. By attitude and implication society will say that if you need something badly enough then it is all right to steal it. It will also imply that if something is lying unused and clearly the owner does not need it, then it is all right to steal it. Society has concluded that if the owner will not miss it because he obviously is not using it and it seems unlikely that he will ever use it again, then it is all right to steal it. On another tack many in society conclude that if the owner of something can afford to buy another then it is all right to steal it. Another prevalent attitude which leads to stealing is that you can take what doesn't belong to you so long as you do that on a small scale. An extension of this is that you can take what doesn't belong to you provided it is from someone you don't know – it may be from the nation in tax or customs duty, or from a public company like the railway, or from your employer whom you seldom, if ever, see, and anyway he has plenty. Public ownership often promotes private irresponsibility. Society frequently implies that stealing is acceptable and even smart so long as you can get away with it.

However, this commandment is absolute and affirms that it is never right to steal, and it affects our attitude towards others' possessions and our attitude towards our own possessions. Let's examine the attitude we need to have towards others' possessions first. The crucial question is to ask why it is wrong to steal from man. The straightforward answer is that God says it is wrong and that should foreclose all discussion. However, it is helpful to unpack that answer at least a little bit and ask why God says so. God says so because stealing is against the laws of honest gain. There are two main ways by which I can legitimately possess things. First of all by working for them and so either possessing them because I have created them with my own hands or because I have earned money to enable me to buy what others have created or what others want to sell for the amount of money I can give them. The other way that I can possess things is by receiving them as a gift freely from the giver. This may come directly or through inheritance. Other ways of getting things are dishonest. The New Testament is practical and direct when it comes to possessions. It says:

Even while we were still there with you, we gave you this rule: 'He who does not work shall not eat'. Yet we hear that some of you are living in laziness, refusing to work, and wasting your time in gossiping. In the Name of the Lord Jesus Christ we appeal to such people – we command them – to quieten down, get to work, and earn their own living (2 Thess 3:10).

Again it says: 'If anyone is stealing he must stop it and begin using those hands of his for honest work so he can give to others in need' (Eph 4:28). Two things are inherent from these two passages about the thief – first, he is living to get rather than to give, and second, he is trying to get something for nothing. When it is recognised that this is what this commandment is about, it is clear that there are a number of ways in which it can be broken.

The commandment is broken by straightforward *thieving*. The bank robber, the burglar, the shop-lifter, and others all come into this category. These obviously infringe this commandment. These are obvious examples of dishonesty. Thieving, however, has a great many first cousins. Sometimes we are prepared to entertain them without fully realising they are so closely connected. So we need to turn the pages of the family album to try to see the likeness and the connection between theft on the one hand and its relations on the other.

One of the close connections of *thieving* is *cheating*. This involves under-paying if you are a customer; over-charging if you are a merchant; rigging the contract if you are in business; beating the customs officials if you are a traveller; and fiddling the tax returns if you are a citizen. Cheating occurs when an employer does not give a fair day's wage for a fair day's work, and equally when an employee does not give a fair day's work for a fair day's wage. I realise that it is difficult to assess these things – and the fees, wages and earnings in the sporting world have made a nonsense of this whole area. However, I used to live in a shipbuilding town where the local economy was built on the contracts that were received and honoured to produce ships. Many who worked there were good, honest citizens who were concerned to build their homes, care for their families and pay their bills. It was with some dismay that I watched a TV documentary programme on the 16th September, 1976 which showed that a shipyard worker in some shipyards would give only between four and five hours work in an eight hour day because of late starting, early finishing and extended breaks, etc. This is cheating. Another area of cheating is an unwillingness or a dilatoriness in the payment of bills. In other words I am content to have in my pocket or my current account at the bank what ought to be in another's pocket or current account. This is cheating and the Eighth Commandment condemns it.

Another close relative of blatant stealing is *gambling*. Some time ago when we were looking at the whole area of money within our church someone was upset when I spoke one Sunday morning about gambling. 'You see,' he said to me, 'I enjoy it and I really spend very little on it. It is heavy-handed and censorious to condemn gambling so categorically'. However, there were two things wrong with what he was saying. First of all the key issue about anything is not whether I enjoy it or not, but whether it is right. The second wrong thing in his reasoning was the 'very little' argument. It is as wrong to steal a penny as it is to steal a pound.

Gambling is three things at one time. It is, first of all, trying to get something for nothing without exchanging – and with no intention of exchanging – any goods or valuables for what you receive. Secondly, it is always trying to gain at someone else's expense. This is perhaps the saddest aspect of gambling for the Christian. It is difficult to imagine how it is possible to love your neighbour and yet to do this to him. Thirdly, gambling is involved when I create a risk of loss which did not exist before. In this regard insurance is not a gamble since it deals with existing risks. When all three things are present, you have a gamble whether the stake is 5p or £500. Sometimes people condemn the Stock Exchange as a gamble. There are circumstances when indeed it is, but it is not so in itself.

In their *Guide to Membership* the Salvation Army define

gambling in the following way: 'Gambling is in essence a form of dishonesty since it consists in trying to obtain from another something for which no return is given'. So gambling infringes the Eighth Commandment and frustrates the reality of the good life. It is by no means a dead issue for us today. The promotion of gambling in one form or another is one of the most powerful and prosperous industries in the country today. Betting is said to employ as many people as those involved in the manufacturing of engineering tools or in the production of textile machinery.

Yet another close relation to thieving is *pilfering*. This is theft from an employer. Thefts at the docks, in shipyards and factories, in public works and offices, is notoriously common. There is a kind of creeping dishonesty in all kinds of work; and the person who is scrupulously honest may well find himself in a small and berated minority. The trouble is that the things involved are often small things – the pencils, rubbers, notepaper, stamps, ash-trays, coat hangers, and so on. But it is symptomatic of a situation in which strict and scrupulous honestly is out of fashion. One of the rarest things in modern society is to carry out the Christian ethic of absolute honesty in a society in which strict honesty has almost ceased to be a virtue. Many people who would be shocked at being identified with people who rob banks, burgle houses, or steal from shops, are, in fact, daily guilty of the fault of annexing property even if it is small and apparently unimportant, to which they have no right. There are few areas of conduct in which the Christian example is more important and more difficult to give.

There are thefts other than the theft of material things that come into this same category. One of these is the theft of time. Again it may be comparatively small in terms of amount, but the reality is there. When a man enters into employment, he also enters into a contract, either written or understood, in which he undertakes to give his employer so much of his time in return for so much pay. He may, for instance, agree to work for eight hours a day. It may well be that, of all thefts, the theft of time is the most common. It is commonplace for people to start late (even though it is only five minutes), and it is almost a universal custom to finish early, and the number of people who do not waste at least some part of the time during which they are supposed to be working is very small indeed. Frequently, when we are working, we do not put our maximum effort into what we are doing. Although it would not be true of every worker there is an attitude in many that their aim is to do as little as possible and to get as much as possible.

One of the problems which confronts a Christian at work is that if he does work hard and as conscientiously as he can, he will almost certainly find that he causes a great deal of trouble. Restriction of work is much more common than encouragement of work, and consequently there is a significant problem here for a Christian which will not be easily solved.

Perhaps the most subtle form of stealing is *borrowing*. There are three kinds of borrower. There is borrowing without asking or informing the owner. Then there is the borrower who forgets that he has borrowed and so he is now in possession of what he has borrowed. Perhaps the most common items that are borrowed are books, umbrellas and garden tools. There may well be a notional intention that after I have read the book or used the tool I will return it, but I never make any real effort to do so. The owner may well struggle on without his own possession assuming that the borrower still needs it. On the other hand he may go to significant effort to seek out the borrower and reclaim what belongs to him. Not infrequently he forgets to whom he lent what he now needs and so is compelled to go out and buy another of the same kind. Finally, there is the borrower who is careless with what he has borrowed. He may lose what he has borrowed or spoil or damage what he has borrowed in some way. He will add insult to injury by returning the borrowed article without getting it repaired and sometimes without apology or explanation. The libraries in Britain lose three and a half million books per year.

Then there is such a thing as stealing a person's *innocence.* There is a kind of person who seduces others into sin. When Robert Burns, the celebrated Scottish poet, went as a young man to Irvine to learn flax-dressing, he fell in with a certain man who taught him a good deal about reckless living. Afterwards Burns said of him: 'His friendship did me a mischief'. How much this man was responsible for the sad life that Burns had, and the hurts in life that he caused others would be difficult to say. However, there are those whose alleged friendship does others a mischief.

It is a simple and tragic fact that the invitation to sin often, perhaps oftenest of all, comes from the invitation of some fellow human being. It is by some so-called friend that a person may receive the initial push that sets him on the pathway to sadness, disillusionment, and heart-break. Jesus makes it quite clear that it is a serious thing to sin yourself, but it is a still more serious thing to teach someone else to sin. 'If anyone should cause one of these little ones to lose faith in me', He says, 'it would be better for that person to have a large mill-stone tied around his neck and be drowned in the deep sea. How terrible for the world that there are things that make people lose their faith! Such things will always happen – but how terrible for the one who causes them!' (Matt 5:6, 7; Mark 9:42; Luke 17:1, 2). Clearly to steal a person's innocence is one of the most serious of sins in the sight of Jesus Christ.

Great controversy and considerable heat is generated over *pollution* in its many forms. This too is a form of stealing. There was a time when landowners planted trees in order that their grandchildren might have the timber. In essence this demonstrates a form of confidence in the future which does not come easily to a generation which looks for quick results. People in the United States today look back with gratitude on decisions made by Theodore Roosevelt in 1907 by which the area of the National Forests was increased from forty-three to a hundred and ninety-four million acres, and their wasteful use restrained by law. But, at the time, no policy of the

Administration excited sharper opposition than the President's efforts on behalf of conservation.

In certain cantons in Switzerland it is an offence to cut down your own tree unless you plant two others in its place. This legislation is based on the conviction that it is immoral to take from the past without giving to the future. There is a cavalier disregard by so many of us to the fact that natural resources such as oil, metals and water, are not limitless. It is not only the 'conservation-fanatics' who are warning about this – now even industrialists and governments may be seen head-in-hands with anxieties over shortage of raw materials. Every motorist knows how quickly the price of his petrol has risen. Western industrial man demands more and more of these resources to feed his technological miracles, and their appetites are insatiable. In the United States a child is born every twelve seconds, a car every five seconds. To keep the car industry growing, cars need to be reasonably rust-prone and so the world's available metal is being used up with prodigal enthusiasm. When each car gets on the road it demands its share of petrol. World consumption of petrol doubles every ten years, so that there is not likely to be any left in the comparatively early part of the twenty-first century.

By then, no doubt some other source of energy will have been processed to cope with this need. Unhappily there is no guarantee of us lasting that long, since we might run out of oxygen before then. A car travelling 625 miles uses up as much oxygen as a man breathes in a year; a jumbo jet burns up 50 tons of oxygen in a single Atlantic crossing. Already the United States produces only sixty per cent of the oxygen it consumes, and if we go on polluting the oceans and thereby killing the oxygen-producing sea plants, we could reach the stage where there is no longer enough oxygen to support human life. Then man will be like a beast of prey who runs out of victims – and starves to death.

How long will we go on plundering the past in order to service and support our present with scant regard to the future?

In view of the widespread nature of stealing it would be helpful to ask and to attempt to answer the question – what causes man to steal? There are fundamentally three causes. First of all – and perhaps most acceptably – man steals because of *necessity*. There comes a point in a man's life when he concludes that his needs are desperate and they can be met in no other way. In fact God recognises this, and requires society to respond to it. In the agrarian society in which His people lived God laid it down that:

> When you gather your crops and fail to bring in some of the corn that you have cut, do not go back for it; it is to be left for the foreigners, orphans, and widows, so that the Lord your God will bless you in everything you do. When you have picked your olives once, do not go back and get those that are left; they are for the foreigners, orphans, and widows. When you have gathered your grapes once, do not go back over the vines a second time; the grapes that are left are for the foreigners, orphans, and widows. Never forget that you were slaves in Egypt; that is why I have given you this command (Deut 24:19–22).

In other words God is concerned to meet the needs of those who are unable to provide for themselves. There is a social responsibility which society must meet. Unhappily in our commercial civilisation there is no equivalent for the ungleaned vineyard and the unbeaten olive tree. The welfare state goes so far, but not far enough. Abuse of the command to respond to the needs of the disadvantaged has always been there, but it is never a reason for society becoming cynical and unresponsive to the needs of her citizens. However pressing necessity might be it is never a justification for theft.

Another cause of stealing is blatant *laziness*. This is a way to get rich without personal effort and industry. Man quickly devises ways for cutting corners and getting things 'on the cheap'. Children cheat in examinations and tests – not out of necessity – but to save themselves the trouble, discipline, application and hours of concentration on work in order to succeed. So they steal the work of others and make claims that it is their own. Thieves often are lazy.

A third cause of stealing is *covetousness.* There is in most of us, not too far beneath the surface of our nature, an acquisitive spirit. We see, are attracted and desire, but know we cannot have. We watch others possess and enjoy what is beyond our reach and ache to possess for ourselves. Somehow we conclude that if only we had that thing some form of happiness would result. We will, of course, deal with this more fully when we come to look at the Tenth Commandment. However, covetousness is a very powerful motive to encourage us to steal.

So much, then, for our attitude towards the possessions of others which motivates theft. Let us turn now to our attitude towards our own possessions. To say yours is mine is to justify stealing from men. To say mine is my own is to justify stealing from God. It is possible to steal from God. If stealing from men clearly shows you have a wrong attitude towards other people's possessions, stealing from God shows you have a wrong attitude towards your own possessions. One of the radical and thrilling evidences that God the Holy Spirit is at work in a human life is not just that a person is now able to speak in tongues and wants to raise his hands in worship, but he has a fundamentally new concept of his possessions. This is a note which is soon struck in the exciting Acts record of the early Church. Luke writes, 'Now the company of those who believed were of one heart and soul, and no one said that any of the things which he possessed was his own, but they had everything in common' (Acts 4:32). Luke goes on to share how powerfully they were able to move and make an impact spiritually because they had come to a new appreciation and understanding of what they possessed materially. The Spirit of God had released them from both acquisitiveness and selfishness and released them in practice and not just in principle to say, 'What is mine is yours' or perhaps more practically to say, 'What is mine is His'. So a completely new dimension of fellowship and relationships was born. It was neither natural nor unnatural – it was completely supernatural, but it had a profoundly tangible effect. The apostle Paul taught clearly and incisively that 'You are not your own; you were bought with a price. So glorify God in your body' (1 Cor 6:19–20). In other words Jesus not only bought me when He gave His sinless life for me on the Cross, He bought me *out*. Every gift and attribute, both physical, natural and spiritual, was paid for by Jesus. He owns me by right and I have no grounds for withholding anything from Him. It was being overwhelmed by this that caused the hymn-writer to sing:

To Thee, Thou bleeding Lamb, I all things owe.
All that I have and am, and all I own.
All that I have is now no longer mine;
And I am not mine own, Lord, I am Thine.

It is possible to steal from God in three ways. First of all when I am careless, insensitive or unfaithful in my stewardship of my *money*. Significantly the Bible is a money-management book. Sixteen out of the thirty-eight parables which Jesus told are money related. Jesus spoke more about money than He did about any other subject – more, for example, than He did about prayer or heaven. Richard Armour writes this poem about money in his book *Going like Sixty*:

Workers earn it,
Spendthrifts burn it,
Bankers lend it,
Women spend it,
Forgers fake it,
Taxes take it,
Dying leave it,
Heirs receive it,
Thrifty save it,
Misers crave it,

Robbers seize it,
Rich increase it,
Gamblers lose it . . .
I could use it.

God certainly uses money to teach us about Himself, about power and authority, about submission and obedience – so many things. The Bible indicates that money is neutral. It is neither good nor bad. It certainly is not dirty! Like sex and politics it is a power which can be used for good or for evil. Money becomes bad only when it dominates our lives and alone determines the direction that our lives are going to take. So Paul writes to young Timothy, 'For the love of money is a source of all kinds of evil. Some have been so eager to have it that they have wandered away from the faith and have broken their hearts with many sorrows' (1 Tim 6:10). The Bible uses poor people, not rich people, to show how to handle money in a proper and godly way. So Jesus illustrates what His heart is declaring and delighting in by a widow giving her offering. Paul uses the poor Macedonian to give a visual aid to other Christians for generous and God-pleasing giving.

The Old Testament is strong in its teaching that where God is concerned we must always put Him first – and we will demonstrate this in the way we handle our material possessions (Hag 1:1–13). Equally the Bible emphasises that only the best is good enough for God (Mal 1:1–4; 3:3–12). It is the New Testament that teaches how important it is to break our conspiracy of silence over our material possessions – this becomes a matter of fellowship (Acts 4:32–35). So it was that Paul writing to these remarkable Christians in Corinth reminds them how rich they are (2 Cor 8:7). They are rich in *faith* – they are great believers and there are many evidences of their faith. They are great *communicators* – their speech and witness cuts a lot of ice. They have a fine *understanding* of the Faith and a sound grasp of the doctrine of God. They are certainly *unselfish* – they are eager always to help others (presumably the old, the young and the disadvantaged). They are rich in *fellowship* with the servants of God – they are warm and concerned and appreciative. Paul is writing to them in a very straightforward way, saying very clearly, 'You can have all of these ennobling and attractive things and yet be reluctant to handle your money in a godly way, and so rob God!'

So he instructs these so rich Corinthians from his experience of the so poor Macedonians. He says first of all that Christians are to give to God *with joy* (8:2). Often in the Christian community the real problem is not shortage of cash, but shortage of joy. Often in the local and national church there is a tenseness and edginess when people are asked to consider how they handle their material resources. All kinds of reasons are cited why this is unnecessary and unacceptable. However, it was said of the early Church that they were always in trouble, but that they were deliriously happy. Secondly, Paul says that these Macedonians gave from *poverty* (8:2). There are two Greek words for poverty – *penes* which referred to a working man who had just enough to keep him going with nothing left over, and *ptochos* which has the idea of crouching and cowering within it, and means destitute and beggared. It is *ptochos* that Paul uses here. There is a lovely story told of the late Joseph Parker, who exercised a powerful preaching ministry in a past generation. A wealthy lady came to him one day and gave him £1 and said: 'The widow's mite'. Parker looked at this well-heeled lady and said: 'Madam, the widow gave two mites!' She went into her handbag and gave him another £1. To this he went on to say – presumably with great courage: 'Madam, the widow gave all that she had!'

Thirdly, says Paul, they gave by *reason* (8:3). He says, 'they gave as much as they could'. In other words it wasn't careless or emotional giving, but they had a 'means test' – they considered how much they had and then computed how much it was reasonable to give. So there was a forthright, careful, honest, realistic and clinical appraisal of their means with a view to that giving. It must always be true that we will never get into the dimension of the supernatural and the impossible until we have begun to operate in the area of the natural and possible as much and as far as we are able to.

Fourthly, the Corinthian Christians are encouraged through the example of the Macedonian Christians to give by *faith* (8:3), having carefully checked the resources that they had. They now were concerned to give not simply out of their own resources, but out of God's resources. There is a whole world of difference between faith and irresponsibility. Paul is not speaking here about foolishness or irresponsibility, but about faith.

Ray and Anne Ortlund in their book *The Best Half of Life* have a remarkable personal story which well illustrates this principle of giving by faith. They write, 'Let your gift to God be the first cheque written every payday, and give until you're a little breathless and dizzy; give through and beyond that pain threshold to the place where, if He doesn't come through, you're sunk. Then you'll know the exhilaration of the faith-life – whatever your income base may be'. Anne writes:

> Through the years as our 10 per cent has doubled and tripled and more, so has the excitement and fun of risking and daring.
>
> Remembering that God talks about tithes 'and offerings', one January first I told Him that in addition to our tithe cheques, every time the offering plate passed, if I had a dollar bill I'd give it whether I thought I needed it or not.
>
> That was such a good year, the next January first I said I'd put in two. Later on, one Sunday night, I put in my last two dollar bills, knowing that the next morning before the banks were open, we had to go across Los Angeles to where we weren't known and take an Australian VIP to breakfast. 'Lord', I prayed, 'please let Ray have breakfast money in his wallet'.
>
> Church ended; we shook the last hands and started across the now deserted parking lot. 'Honey', I said, 'I hope you have money for breakfast'.

'No', he said, 'I was so blessed, I put in my last five dollars.'

Just then, lying on the parking lot pavement in front of us, all neatly folded up in a square, was a ten-dollar bill!

The next evening we happened to be taking Lorrayne, Ray's secretary, to dinner and we told her how God had fed our Australian breakfast that morning.

Lorrayne looked simply incredulous. 'That was my ten dollars!' she said. 'It fell out of my shoe and I almost cried. Then I asked the Lord to have someone who needed it find it.'

(By this time we'd gotten more cash at the bank and we handed the ten dollars back.)

Out of all the hundreds of people who had walked across the parking lot that night, God had ordained to let Lorrayne lend us ten dollars for twenty-four hours – to increase both her faith and ours!

Fifthly, the Macedonian Christians gave by *begging* (8:4). Normally we associate the word 'begging' with getting rather than with giving, but here 'they begged us and pleaded for the privilege of having a part in helping God's people in Judea'. They begged to give rather than to get. There is all the difference between the way that the world normally gives and the way the Christian normally gives – for the Christian giving is a delight and not a duty. It is the expression of love and not the result of the enforcement of law. The practical attitude of the Christian is not so much formed by asking how much of my money shall I give to God as it is by asking how much of God's money shall I keep for myself in order to maintain honour in my relationships and my responsibilities. The example in all of this, of course, is our Lord Jesus Himself. It is of Him that Paul writes as he summarises what he has been saying, 'I am not laying down any rules. But by showing how eager others are to help, I am trying to find out how real your own love is. You know the grace of our Lord Jesus Christ; rich as He was, He made Himself poor for your sake, in order to make you rich by means of His poverty'.

R. B. James says that, 'the money retained in the hands of God's people and which God owns and claims is a most potent hindrance to a living and strong spirituality'. It is surprising how much space is given to money in Scripture – how we get it; how we save it; and how we use it. It is always revealing to see a person's reactions to his possessions – whether he is rich or poor.

When we give money to God, we are not really giving something which is ours to Him, but rather giving something which is His to Him. The real question is not how much of my money should I give to God, but how much of God's money should I keep for myself. When my children were young and they gave me a present for my birthday or at Christmas, what they gave would normally be given as a result of money that I had originally given them. That did not in any way detract from the wonder of their gift. It did not occur to me to think, 'They are only giving me what is mine anyway'. Neither does God.

It still fills me with wonder that I received a letter some years ago from a young woman called Christine. £43 was enclosed with the letter, payable to the church. She explained that some years previously before she had left us prior to her marriage, she had covenanted before God to give £100. She had only given £80. She had spent the other £20 on perfectly legitimate things. However, she felt that she had 'stolen' from God and needed to put it right. The £43 represented the £20 still to be honoured, and since it was six years later she had added on an extra £23 to cover interest and inflation. I have no idea how she computed that extra £23 – and I really did not care. I was moved by it – and I feel sure that God loved her for it!

Secondly, I am stealing from God when I am careless and insensitive in my stewardship of my *time*. How much of God's work is hindered by people saying 'I haven't time!' The fact is that Jesus was able to say at the end of His short – and for the most part ordinary and uneventful – life, 'I have finished the work you have given me to do'. What a wonderful thing to come to the end of life – whether it is long or short – and to be able to conclude that I have fulfilled all that God had in mind for me not simply in terms of time, but in terms of eternity. One tenth of a week is approximately seventeen hours – approximately two working days of eight hours each. So even a legal requirement computed on the basis of the Old Testament title releases quite a number of hours for God. But the Christian is not motivated by law, but by love. His concern is not 'How much of my time is God going to get?' but rather, 'How much of His time am I allowed to have to do the things I need/want to do?' We need to take stock of our time carefully to ensure that we do not use it selfishly, impulsively and under the tyranny of the urgent. My task is to find out what the will of God is for my life not only generally, but as a daily discipline and then follow that will in order to be able to finish it. Persuasively Paul writes to the Ephesian Christians, 'It is God Himself who has made us what we are and given us new lives in Christ Jesus; and long ages ago He planned that we should spend these lives in helping others' (Eph 2:20). In my growing up years there was a hymn that was often sung in our church, and it became familiar to me. We do not base our theology on the hymnbook, but one part of that hymn is a good practical basis on which to secure our lives:

> There's a work for Jesus ready at your hand;
> 'Tis a work the Master just for you has planned.
> Haste to do His bidding; yield Him service true;
> There's a work for Jesus none but you can do.

If ever there was a need to bring anything under the Lordship of Christ it is the time that we have available – time entrusted to us by God. How we need to be daily filled with the Holy Spirit to enable us to be faithful stewards of this precious commodity.

Confronted by the fruitful and relevant ministry of D. L. Moody, one critical opponent of Moody said, 'Does Mr Moody think he has a monopoly of the Holy Spirit?' To this one of

Moody's defenders replied, 'No, but the Holy Ghost seems to have a monopoly of Mr Moody'. Just so. How much we need to live governed lives – under the Lordship of Christ and sustained by the fullness of His Spirit. It was John Wesley who declared: 'I want a bunch of God-intoxicated men and I will turn England upside down'. He got them, and he did!

Thirdly, I steal from God when I withhold my *talents* from Him. The Bible makes it crystal clear that literally no one is without at least one gift from God. Jesus makes it clear in His teaching that the man with one talent who does not use it for the benefit of his master, but goes and hides it away is in fact robbing his master. God invests gifts in us because He is looking for interest which will accrue as a result of our using what He has given. This is not an option that we have – it is our obligation.

It is possible to use for ourselves money, time and talents that really belong to God. This is stealing in the same way as using for our own benefit things which really belong to others. We may well condemn the latter and yet in practice condone the former.

The good life will consist of ensuring that both God and man not only get their due, but are also recipients of the supernatural love that has been released in our hearts by the Holy Spirit. In any case I do not need to steal since:

> Jesus Christ is made to me all I need, all I need;
> He alone is all my plea – He is all I need.
> Wisdom, righteousness and power – holiness this very hour;
> My redemption full and sure – He is all I need.

This is not spiritual escapism, this is practical reality.

~ 10 ~

My word!

There are two ways in which this Ninth Commandment is related to the others. First of all it has to do with *stealing* every bit as significantly as the Eighth Commandment. The Eighth Commandment has to do with stealing property – and that we recognise easily and immediately. The Seventh Commandment has to do with stealing a man or a woman's partner. The Sixth Commandment has to do with stealing another's life, and robbing him of what can never be returned or replaced. The Tenth Commandment is stealing from others with your mind – and it is there that most difficulties begin. However, you can steal from people with your tongue – and this is what the Ninth Commandment is all about! The Eighth Commandment deals with dishonest speech. So in the second half of the Ten Commandments there is a great deal of instruction not to take from another what does not belong to you. God wants, of course, to set us free in deed, in thought, and in word, to give rather than to take.

The theft of a person's character and good name is an awesome thing. The recklessness with which people repeat stories about other people without ever checking them is an astonishing thing. There seems to be something in human nature which takes a delight in hearing, and then often in repeating, what is discreditable to others. It is so easy to start a story, and so difficult to stop it. The proverb says that there are three things which never come back, the spent arrow, the lost opportunity and the spoken word. It is certainly true that there is no more serious wrong that we can do to any man than to rob him of his good name. It is worth requoting Shakespeare's Iago in *Othello*:

> Good name in man and woman, dear my Lord,
> Is the immediate jewel of their souls.
> Who steals my purse, steals trash; 'tis something, nothing;
> 'Twas mine, 'tis his and has been slave to thousands;
> But he that filches from me my good name
> Robs me of that which naught enriches him,
> And makes me poor indeed.

To listen to the malicious story is almost, if not quite, as bad as to repeat it. Stop stealing a man's character!

The second way in which the Ninth Commandment is related to the other nine is that the first part of the Ten Commandments have to do with my relationship to God, whilst the second part of the Ten Commandments have to do with my relationship to men. In each of these parts there is a commandment which has to do directly with the tongue. The First Commandment (Exod 20:3) has to do with my head—and what I believe. The Second Commandment (Exod 20:4–6) has to do with my hands—and how I behave. The Third Commandment (Exod 20:7) has to do with my mouth—and how I speak about God. The Ninth Commandment (Exod 20:16) has to do with my mouth—and how I speak about man. In other words it is not only man who can be a victim of the human tongue—God can be too! God's honour and man's reputation need to be guarded in the way we speak.

Although we do not, the Bible does take sins of the tongue very seriously. We tend to rationalise, excuse, spiritualise or in some other way treat our words very lightly. We even have a little ditty which is taught from earliest childhood that, 'Sticks and stones could break my bones, but names will never hurt me!' To write these words is to recall incidents from the school playground where a child has been vilified verbally and is now replying in the only way open to him. The ditty is, of course, quite untrue. Names we are called and words which are used against us hurt and wound us very deeply. Indeed, it is my perception that it is easier to bear physical assault than it is to bear verbal assault in a civilised society.

Jesus never left us in any doubt as to how seriously He regarded the words that we use and those which are used against us. He said, in fact, that we will be justified or condemned by our words. 'I tell you this,' He said, 'that you must give an account on Judgment Day for every idle word you speak. Your words now reflect your fate then; either you will be justified by them or you will be condemned' (Matt 12:36, 37). Equally, in that powerful final word at the end of the New Testament, John declares from heaven and from the heart of Jesus that 'cowards who turn back from following me, and those who are unfaithful to me, and the corrupt and murderers, and the immoral, and those conversing with demons, and idol worshippers, and *all liars* – their doom is in the lake that burns with fire and sulphur – This is the second death' (Rev 21:7).

Why is it that the Bible takes words so seriously? It is because justice is impossible without truth. God is clearly revealed in the Bible as the God of justice. Equally God is revealed as the God of truth. In our exploration of the Sixth Commandment we noted that we would only ever be able to understand the Bible's teaching on life when we understood that it clearly values justice as more important than human life.

In a law court justice cannot be done until truth is established. Lies will always cause the guilty to go free and the innocent to suffer. Because God is a God of justice then He must demand truth. Justice and truth belong together. Truth is one of those words which we use freely without fully understanding what is meant by it. Biblically it has both a Hebrew and a Greek origin. So far as Hebrew is concerned, it has the idea of firmness about it. Truth is something which you can lean on and it will not collapse – it will bear your weight. In winter when a pond freezes over it is sometimes necessary to put a 'danger' notice on one part of it. The whole surface looks the same, and the skater may well assume that every bit of it is the same, but the notice is a reminder that this is not so, and there is a part which will not bear his weight. This is the opposite of truth. Truth, by its very nature is as it seems, and it will never let you down, and will always bear your weight when you have to trust it and lean on it and depend on it. So far as the Greeks were concerned truth had the idea of something which was not hidden. It had no shadows and could bear exposure to the brightest and most searching light. Firmness and openness are two fundamental characteristics of truth.

The relevance of this commandment for us is seen first of all in a court of law. 'Do not accuse anyone falsely' is repeated in the same form in English in Deuteronomy 5:20. Although the English translation is the same in both cases, the Hebrew is different. In the Exodus version the meaning is *lying* or *untrue*; in the Deuteronomy version the meaning is *insincere*, *empty*, *frivolous*. The meaning is not essentially different, but it might be said that the Exodus version thinks rather of the nature of the evidence and the Deuteronomy version thinks of the spirit in which it is given.

This commandment was originally a forensic commandment and dealt with the obligations of a witness in a court of law. The Hebrews had a horror of false accusation – as we ought to have – and again and again it is grimly and seriously condemned. For the Psalmist the bitterest thing of all is that false and malicious witnesses rise up against him (Ps 27:12; 35:11). Repeatedly the wise man of the book of Proverbs condemns false accusation (Prov 6:19; 12:17; 14:5; 19:5; 19:9; 19:28; 21:28; 25:18). In the New Testament false witness or accusation is one of the sins which come out of the evil heart of man (Matt 15:19). False accusation is given at both the trials of Stephen (Acts 6:13) and Jesus (Matt 26:59, 60).

In all civilised countries the bearing of false witness or the wilful giving of false evidence under oath or perjury is always regarded as a most serious offence. The fact is that if people are allowed to get away with it then the whole foundation of justice would be hopelessly undermined. A person's reputation, and perhaps even his fate, would be in the hands of any unscrupulous person who chose to misrepresent him and tell lies about him.

Although it is now possible simply to give an affirmative only, the oath that is given is to 'swear by Almighty God to tell the truth, the whole truth, and nothing but the truth'. That oath indicates that truth can be perverted in two ways. I can pervert the truth either by telling less than the whole truth or I can pervert the truth by telling more than the whole truth, and *both* are wrong! Either way I am being a false witness, and, in fact, being guilty of perjury. Truth is never to be anything less than it is and it is never to be any more than it is. I am not allowed to embellish it with my own opinions, thoughts or imagination. When I do this then the truth is no longer what it seems to be – and so is no longer truth.

Secondly, however, this commandment has a relevance in the community as well as in a court of law. We may never have been in a witness box giving evidence, and some never will be, and yet we give evidence every day as we go about our ordinary routine responsibilities. Every one of us has talked about someone else sometime. What we have said about them has made them be treated, thought of, or talked about either fairly or unfairly by the person to whom we spoke. People have formed an opinion about them in the light of what we have said. In this sense every one of us has given and will give evidence in the community.

Gossip is a word with an interesting history. Today, to call someone a gossip, is to risk their friendship or indeed any meaningful relationship. Five hundred years ago to be a gossip was to be complimented. Originally gossip had a 'd' in it (i.e. godship). It meant that you had a godly and prayerful concern for other people. In a service for the baptism of an infant, godparents were asked, 'Are you willing to be godships for this child?' (i.e. 'Will you take a godly and prayerful interest in him/her?'). The word then became 'gossip'. But even then it had a good meaning. It described someone who would gossip to God and pray for people. The word then became used for taking a friendly interest in others. In Shakespeare's *Henry V* two soldiers are discussing their hopes and fears on the eve of the Battle of Agincourt. They describe each other not as 'pals' or 'mates' or 'buddies', but as 'gossips' (i.e. 'you are my gossip'). From there, however, it declined into something which was nasty, hurtful and unacceptable. George MacDonald describes a gossip as 'a beast of prey which does not wait for the death of the creature which it devours'. Pascal observes, 'If everyone knew what everyone said about the other, there would not be left four friends in the world'. Gossip became a destructive and wounding thing. It is a sobering thought that very few of us – if any – would be happy to have everything we have said about someone else told to them.

Gossip has a quality about it which makes it difficult to heal and to put right properly what has been said. During World War I a large quantity of blue cross gas was manufactured in a munitions factory near Cologne in Germany. The city fathers were concerned to destroy it after the War was over. They were troubled by its dangerous possibilities. They tried to burn it, but the fumes affected vegetation and the lungs of the population for many miles around. They tried to bury it, but they became afraid that it would affect the sub-soil water and contaminate not only the water used for animal and human consumption, but also the land where it was buried. They thought they might sink it at sea, but there was an outcry that it was far too dangerous to transport it down the Rhine. As the years passed it was neutralised, burned, buried, disinterred, and re-buried. Whatever they did the city custodians were troubled by it. Today it is in a vast concrete coffin in the Wahner Moor and for well over half a century the Moor has been closed to the public. To make poison gas is not too difficult, but to destroy it satisfactorily, or to render it harmless in one way or another, has proved almost impossible, and that has defeated the ingenuity of the experts.

Gossip is a bit like that. It is not difficult to speak carelessly and inaccurately about someone. Most of us would be guilty of this at some time or another. To mend what has been done as a result of gossip is much more difficult.

The story goes that there was once a woman who could not control her tongue. She knew it and was very worried about it. She went to a wise man and asked for his help and advice. He said to her, 'Here's a goose; I want you to walk home with it in your arms; as you go I want you to pluck it and to scatter its feathers broadcast. When you have done that come back immediately to me'. She did so and she came back. 'What do I do now?' she asked. 'Now', said the wise man, 'I want you to go back along the road and to gather up all the feathers you plucked and scattered.' 'But', she said, 'that is impossible. The wind has scattered the feathers far and wide and I can never get them back.' 'Exactly' said the wise man, 'Your words are like that. Once you have spoken them they are scattered broadcast and you can never get them back.' Once spoken, words are often irretrievable. Physically, when we speak our words make waves in the atmosphere just as a stone thrown into the pool of water. However, there is no end to the atmosphere. In other words every word that we have ever spoken is somewhere in the universe going on and on for ever and ever. Some day God is going to collect all our words and we are going to give account for them. Not only do our words affect the lives of people physically, but in much deeper ways the effect of our words goes on and on psychologically, morally, socially and spiritually.

This is why the Ninth Commandment is so relevant to us. First of all, unless it is obeyed the course of justice is defeated and so the innocent suffer and the guilty go free. Secondly, false accusations often defy every attempt to destroy the damage they have caused.

How do we break this commandment? First of all by telling blatant, obvious and outright lies. Almost proverbially George Washington had the reputation of never having told a lie. To the query about the apple tree which no longer was in an upright condition, he is reputed to have said, 'Father, I cannot tell a lie. I did it with my little hatchet'. This incident is always told to illustrate Washington's life of absolute honesty. If indeed this is so then probably he is the only one who has avoided this prevalent and contagious disease. The Authorised Version (Ps 116:11) states quite baldly, 'All men are liars'. Jesus, in speaking to the Pharisees about His own relationship to the Father, says of them 'You are of your father the devil, and your will is to do your father's desires. He was a murderer from the beginning, and has nothing to do with the truth, because there is no truth in him . . .' (John 8:44).

Lying seems to be something which is second nature to man; it is ingrained and inborn and has got to the centre and core and essence of life. You never have to teach a child to tell lies. It instinctively knows how to do it. The Psalmist says, 'Evil men go wrong all their lives; they tell lies from the day they are born' (58:3) and 'you take pleasure in lies' (62:4). The prophets condemn it – Isaiah 9:15; 59:3, 4; Jeremiah 9:3; 14:14; 23:25, 26, 32; 27:10, 14, 16, 18; Hosea 10:13; Amos 2:4. There are frequent threats and warnings to those who practise falsehood and lying – Isaiah 28:17; Psalms 63:11 and 101:7. In the New Testament the Book of Revelation categorically declares that everyone who loves or practises falsehood will be shut out from the presence of God – 21:27; 22:15. Lying is seen in the Bible as something which profanes God (Ezek 13:17–19) and dishonours man (Ps 119:69).

One of the most interesting things in the prophets is to see the things in company with which lying is mentioned and rebuked. Murder and loot accompany lies in Nahum 3:1. Adultery and encouragement to do wrong accompany lies in Jeremiah 23:14. Misgovernment results from lying in Proverbs 29:12. Lying brings a whole range of companions with it.

The biblical evidence indicates that lying was and is a prevalent sin and how God through His prophets and wise men set His heart against it. There are three closely interconnected New Testament Greek words in this whole context.

Diabolos, which means 'a slanderer' is one of the things women are forbidden to be in 1 Timothy 3:11. There is the word *blasphemia*, which, when it is used in regard to God, means 'blasphemy', and when it is used in regard to men means 'insulting slander'. It is one of the sins forbidden to the Christian in Ephesians 2:31. Then there is *katalalia*, which the King James Version translates 'backbiting' and 'evil-speaking' in 2 Corinthians 12:20 and 1 Peter 2:1. The RSV translates it 'slander'. It is significant that there are so many Greek words for this kind of sin. Presumably the number of words shows how prevalent the thing was – and is. There can be few sins which are more terrible in their effect, for this sin of the malicious lie can ruin faith in God and destroy character and kill friendship with man.

Secondly, we break this commandment by deception – that is, by giving an impression of something which is not true. That can be true of circumstances, but it can be even more devastatingly true of people. The classic case of Jacob pretending to be Esau in order to get Esau's birthright and blessing from his father stands as a good example of this.

Some years ago a young Egyptian doctor came into our lives and into our home. He came to work as an obstetrician and gynaecologist in the maternity hospital in the town where we lived. For the years he was there he really became a member of our family. He was hoping to take a qualification in Edinburgh University which would enable him to practise as a consultant obstetrician and gynaecologist. Zichri was a fine Christian and came from a very active Christian home in Cairo where his father was responsible for leading a mission. He told us a story once of his young boyhood when a lady visitor arrived at their home. His father was out and his mother received the guest warmly. She sat her down in their sitting room and instructed Zichri to look after her while she went and made some tea. When Zichri's mother returned she found a somewhat distraught guest in the sitting room with Zichri. When his mother enquired what was wrong, the guest was only too willing to explain. 'Your son', she said, 'has walked round and round me staring intently at me all the time, and never saying a word.' 'Why were you doing that?' demanded the mother. Zichri remained tight-lipped and refused to reply. 'You owe our guest an explanation and an apology,' she insisted. At last the pressurised Zichri decided to explain. 'Well', he said, 'father and you have often spoken of this lady as being two-faced, and I was looking for the other face that you spoke of.' The upset and offended guest left and relationships between her and the leader of the mission and his wife were never quite the same again. The situation is not at all unfamiliar in Christian circles.

We can appear to be to others what we are not. We can give an impression of godliness which is far from the truth. Often how we appear in church and with our Christian friends is not quite how we appear at home and with the family.

Another way to break this commandment is through exaggeration. Few would begrudge the good story-teller the right to embroider and embellish what he has to say. No-one is apt to take him too seriously when he is telling the story for our entertainment. However, the trouble arises when he does not check the habit when talking about people or giving details of a situation where accuracy is of the essence of the account. There are two kinds of exaggeration. Real enthusiasm often leads to exaggeration and this is usually quite harmless. But exaggeration can be dangerous when superlatives and absolutes are used recklessly, such as, 'He's never on time' or 'she always nags me' or 'they are completely wrong' or 'they are all against me'. There is an inherent danger in using these absolute words—never, completely, always, all. A wrong impression can be conveyed either about another or about yourself.

Exaggeration can sometimes be destructive to faith—either by exaggerating the size of the problem or by exaggerating the poverty of our faith. When Jesus and the disciples were confronted by the crowd of 5,000 which required to be fed, Jesus instructed the disciples to make the crowd sit down in groups of hundreds and groups of fifties.

Jesus was concerned to know the size of the problem which confronted them – and He wanted to know the size with accuracy. In that same incident the disciples concluded they had nothing with which to respond to this immense challenge, and Jesus had to help them to understand that they had – they had a little boy's picnic lunch. With little, Jesus taught them how to respond to the need which was now precisely before them.

Fourthly, we break this commandment by covering up. Again, the Bible provides us with a classic illustration of this. 2 Samuel 11 tells the awesome story of King David's adultery with Bathsheba and the murder of her husband Uriah. The following chapter (2 Sam 12:1–7) records the parable which Nathan told as God's messenger sent by the Lord to David. As a result of hearing Nathan's parable which David thought was true, it says that 'David became very angry at the rich man and said, "I swear by the living Lord that the man who did this ought to die! For having done such a cruel thing he must pay back four times as much as he took". "You are that man", Nathan said to David ...' Often the things which annoy us most easily are the very things of which we ourselves are guilty. Often the people who irritate us are showing the very traits of character that we have to deal with in our own hearts and experience.

Covering up is not unusual and often is the instinctive reaction that we have to the clear possibility of being found out when we are in the wrong.

Half-truths are another form of deception because half-truths are fundamentally half-lies. In some ways a deliberate lie is not quite so dangerous as a half-truth. What we say is accurate, but what we don't say – although we know it perfectly well – gives a totally false impression. A half-truth is often bordering on insinuation. The story is told of a first mate who often became drunk and incapable of carrying out his responsibilities aboard ship. He was warned by the captain that if it happened once more the offence would be recorded in the ship's log. Inevitably it happened. The captain kept his word, and wrote in the ship's log: 'Tuesday March 14. First mate drunk'. This really hurt the old sailor and in his shame he vowed he would take vengeance. He did. Two days later he sneaked into the captain's quarters and wrote in the ship's log, 'Thursday, March 16. Captain is sober today'.

Insinuation and innuendo is subtle and dangerous and, in fact, cowardly. We can practise this when we ask suggestive questions. For instance, 'Do you think John has been faithful to his wife?' (with the emphasis of tone on the 'you' or on the 'faithful'). Or we can ask, 'Do you think he really means it?' Insinuation can defame a man's character. We do it with sarcastic name-dropping: 'Oh, John!' we say with a smile or a grunt. Or, 'Haven't you met John yet? You will!' Our tone of voice can so easily make us a false witness. So can our silence. We can insinuate a person's guilt when he is accused in our presence and we know him to be innocent, but lack the courage to rise to his defence. In so doing our silence very often confirms the condemnation of the accuser.

Sixthly, make-believe can convey truth which in fact has no foundation in reality and so mislead. The world of fantasy has a significant part to play in the development of a child. The majority of a child's 'playing' takes him into a make-believe world. That is not only acceptable, but also necessary. Tragedy occurs, however, when that is continued into adult life and can have serious consequences. The French emperor, Napoleon, had a facility for reckoning on whole divisions of troops that did not even exist on paper far less in fact when he was in real trouble. Fantasy thinking can cause great danger whenever it is practised.

Another form of conveying the wrong impression is the cloaking of what I feel and believe under the guise of 'they are saying'. Often 'they are saying' really means 'I think' or 'I am disturbed' or 'I am upset' or 'I do not like'. It is cowardly and yet again conveys a totally wrong impression among those to whom we are speaking. It is always easier to state my negative and unpleasant conclusions as from the lips of others rather than my own.

Finally we break this commandment when we accuse not only our neighbour falsely, but when we accuse ourselves falsely. It is not at all uncommon for people, sometimes as a result of inverted pride, to cut themselves down to almost nothing and ostentatiously parade their mistakes and shortcomings as often as possible. It seems to be a dramatic display of humility—but often causes the opposite reaction. Most people are better than they think they are. Most are loved, esteemed and respected by more people than they know of. Many have a personal identity crisis, and whilst it is important not to be unreal about oneself, nevertheless we need constantly to remember who we are in God. God has created us, redeemed us, filled us with His spirit, given us gifts both natural and spiritual, ordained a purpose for our lives before He ever created the world and presents us with opportunities to become what He always wanted us to be.

Centuries ago the scholar Muretus became ill when walking in the streets of his city. Abject poverty was the normal accompaniment of the scholastic life and food and warmth often had to be sacrificed. He was taken to a hospice unconscious and in a poor condition through under-nourishment. Two surgeons examined him as he came to consciousness again. They viewed the skeletal body and the threadbare ragged clothing and obviously took him for a worthless beggar. The language of the educated was Latin and it was in that language that they spoke to each other and conveyed their conclusion that since Muretus was only a destitute beggar there was nothing they needed to do for him or wanted to do for him. Their whole conversation about him was demeaning and off-hand. Muretus heard their conversation since they had no idea that he understood every word they spoke. At last he spoke and said to both the doctors (in Latin!) 'Call no man worthless for whom Christ died!' Just so, we need to maintain and demonstrate with a quiet, unpretentious dignity the reality of our salvation lest we convey to others less than is real about ourselves as a result of the grace of God and the enabling power of God.

Never belittle, underrate or insult the Lord's own creation and redemption.

In view of the multiplicity of ways that we can break the Ninth Commandment, how are we to respond to it? First of all we need to understand clearly the source of all falsehood. We need to appreciate why we are as we are – for it is never necessary to teach a child how to lie. Having felt perfectly healthy we may suddenly come down with a miserable, heavy cold within a matter of hours. In this situation we normally ask, 'Where in the world did I pick up this cold?' We recall the past day or two and think of possible sources of infection. So it ought to be with falsehood. The fact of the matter is that we got it from our father – not our Heavenly Father nor our earthly father, but the other one. Jesus, in a tough question-and-answer session says, 'You are the children of your father, the Devil, and you want to follow your father's desires. From the very beginning he was a murderer and has never been on the side of truth, because there is no truth in him. When he tells a lie, he is only doing what is natural to him, because he is a liar and the father of all lies' (John 8:44). There are certain traits of character which we become aware of and they clearly reflect our human heredity – 'like father like son'. This is true also in a spiritual sense, and we reflect to a greater or a lesser extent the character of the one in whose bondage we are born. This is why it is so necessary for us to recognise our need of personal salvation. We need to know that God wants to transfer us from the Kingdom of Darkness into the Kingdom of His dear Son – so that we will be free to live in righteousness by the power of God's Holy Spirit. Then and only then do we have any hope of being separated from and delivered from the effect and influence of the devil upon our lives.

Right from the very beginning the devil's subtle deception began to operate. In the record of our first parents his clever approach to Eve was to cause her to question God's word. He says to her: 'Did God really tell you not to eat fruit from any tree in the garden?' So he introduces doubt, uncertainty and more than a touch of ridicule. 'We may eat the fruit of any tree in the garden', the woman answered, 'except the tree in the middle of it. God told us not to eat the fruit of that tree or even touch it; if we do we will die.' Then the devil's subtlety disappears and he takes a direct route to confuse, and contradict God. 'The snake replied, "That's not true; you will not die . . ."' So the deterioration sets in and doubt leads to disobedience and disobedience leads to spiritual darkness – and that spiritual darkness could only ultimately be penetrated by the One who came as the light of the world.

The incident is followed by another incident where Adam has learned quickly the art of twisting truth. 'That evening they heard the Lord God walking in the garden, and they hid from him among the trees. But the Lord God called out to the man, "Where are you?" He answered, "I heard you in the garden; I was afraid and hid from you, because I was naked."' True, indeed, since he was naked, but that was not the cause of his fear. He was afraid because he had been disobedient.

In the very next chapter of the book of Genesis we read, 'Then Cain said to his brother Abel, "Let's go out in the fields." When they were out in the fields, Cain turned on his brother and killed him. The Lord asked Cain, "Where is your brother Abel?" He answered, "I don't know. Am I supposed to take care of my brother?"' So lying and falsehood and duplicity are quickly established and the devil has infected the human race.

We need to be careful lest we glamorise the devil. Often the way we speak of him can convey an impression which suggests he is a comic figure and not quite real. John Brown of Haddington spoke of him as 'His Satanic Majesty'. Billy Bray, the Cornish evangelist whom God used so powerfully, spoke of him as 'Old Smutty Face'. Even C. S. Lewis, the strong antagonist of the Christian Faith who was to become one of its clearest and most forthright apologists speaks of him as 'Our Father Below'. There is a benignity about this which can soften the reality and deadly nature of his work. The Bible uses a multiplicity of names for him – and Bible names, with a few exceptions, describe the people who bear them. In the Bible he is called *Satan* which means an 'adversary'. His mission is to oppose God's perfect will and purpose and to attempt to frustrate man's sincerest responses to the love, grace and providence of God. He is the *devil* or 'slanderer' or 'destroyer'. He slanders God to man and communicates the lies to man that God does not really love us, nor does He have the power to rescue or help us. He slanders man to God and indicates that a man does not love God for His own sake, but only for what he can get out of God. He is *Belial*, the low, abject one; and this needs little help in understanding. He is the Wicked One; the God of this World; the Prince of Darkness; the Dragon; the Tormentor; the Accuser; the Deceiver; the Liar; the Murderer; he has the power of death; the Tempter. There is nothing even mildly amusing about these names. Many of them convey his ability and willingness and desire to deceive and destroy. Deception and destruction, then, are his territory.

This honoured high-ranking, attractive angelic being had, in the words of Martin Luther, a 'hideous fall from heaven to hell'. We do not know when this occurred, but obviously it was prior to time, in eternity. Whenever it was, he who was among the greatest of God's angels fell to become the Wicked One, the Enemy of God and the Deceiver of God's people. His ultimate downfall is certain because one of the reasons Jesus came to earth was to destroy him (Heb 2:14 and 1 John 3:8). However, we are foolish and unrealistic if we underestimate his present reality and ability. The fact that he is a fallen angel is a reference to his wickedness and in no way suggests that he has lost spiritual power, or is less likely to attack us. He will attempt to intrude upon our physical condition, creating physical pressure, pain and anxiety. He will attempt to undermine our belief and erode the simplicity and certainty of our convictions. He will attempt to minimise and neutralise the importance of our moral choices and the resulting effect on our standards and behaviour.

How important it is for us to recognise that on every

occasion when we willingly move into areas of deception and falsehood, either by the things we say or the way we live, we are submitting to the devil's influence, manipulation and ministry, giving him a landing pad on which he can find a foothold in our lives and offering him territory which he can claim. This is not to exonerate us nor free us from personal responsibility. We, as Christians, have the God-given ability now to choose what is right and true, and in the supernatural power of the Holy Spirit to walk in righteousness and truth.

In Charles Reade's novel *The Cloister and the Heath* the hero's friend tries to cheer him up by saying from time to time 'Courage, comrade, the devil is dead'. From what has been said that clearly is not true. Although his ultimate defeat is certain, he is not dead yet. Our hope lies not in a devil who is dead, but in a God who is vibrantly alive. Our natural inclinations are to make us want victory without any confrontation. True victory is to be found where the devil is most active – and for most such a place is where the temptation to falsehood, hyprocrisy and deception is strongest. It is in the place of temptation that God wants to give us victory. Not only do we need to recognise the source of all falsehood, but we also need to realise the stubborn, persistent faithfulness of our deliverer.

One day there came into the world for the first time One who told the truth, the whole truth and nothing but the truth. He came declaring in the simplest way, but with the most profound implications 'I am the Truth'. Jesus never used flattery, because flattery is false witness *for* someone and not *against* him. Jesus never used falsehood – because falsehood presents people and situations in a bad light – against anyone. So neither flattery nor falsehood were ever His style. As He dealt with others, so He dealt with Himself – He neither used flattery nor falsehood in His claims about Himself, even through modesty. When He speaks of Himself as 'the Truth' there is something firm, uncomplicated and dependable there.

So we can bring these spoiled lives of ours – spoiled by lies and falsehood – and ask Him to deal with them. The devil does two things with sin – he magnifies it or he minimises it. He will tell you either that your sin is too big to be dealt with and you are stuck with it for the rest of your life, or else he will insist or infer that a sin like lying is only natural, everybody else does it, and it doesn't matter anyway. One way or the other, he will leave things as they are, and the effect and influence of the sin continues. Of no other sin is this more true than lying. God, on the other hand, does two things with sin too. He deals with it and then dismisses it. He is willing and, indeed, wanting, not only to forgive our sin, but also to forget it. It is on the basis always, however, of our repentance.

We need to recognise that lying is not something to be trifled with or excused – however natural we have concluded it is. We dare not excuse it or condone it in the lives of others nor in our own life. How easy it is to do this – even in the words we use. A 'fib' is a lie and there is no such thing as a white lie – ever. We need to call accusing someone falsely what it is in God's sight – sin. God has said so, and the first step in repentance is agreeing with God and calling sin (whatever form it takes) what He calls it.

Secondly, I need to feel as God feels about it in my heart. According to God's standards falsehood in any of its forms shares with pride the unpleasant destruction of being a very direct road to perdition. Falsehood will have no place whatsoever in God's eternal kingdom. It is the very antithesis of all that God is and stands for. I can be sure that God hates falsehood with a holy zeal. I need to ask the Holy Spirit to enable me to feel the depth of feeling which is in God's heart against it.

Thirdly, I need to confess it with my mouth. Maybe that would be in private quietly before God. Often it helps, however, to confess things with which we struggle constantly to another or to others. It seems that the only way sin leaves the body is through the mouth. Something happens to sin not only when I recognise it in my heart, but when I confess it with my mouth. Verbalising it in confession audibly is part of the way to victory over it.

Fourthly, I need to set a guard over my lips and determine that they will only speak now what is truth. I need to exercise my will over this damning thing. God not only wants to forgive my sin, but to set me free to live a righteous life. Honesty, accuracy of speech, wanting the best and showing another in the very best light is all part of righteous living and is characteristic of the good life. The moment I determine to do this rather than detract from someone and exalt myself by putting him down, the Holy Spirit comes quickly to my aid to strengthen my will.

Fifthly, it may well be necessary to go to the person against whom I have spoken and with whom I have been unfair and ask his forgiveness. Few sins require restitution more than the sin of accusing anyone falsely. The devil will insist that to do so will forever ruin a relationship. It may well do this, but normally it will provide an even stronger basis for fellowship than ever before. Trust in one another and transparency before one another is fundamental to the whole biblical concept of fellowship. It is into this real and strong relationship with one another that God wants to bring us.

This is the only way we are ever going to manage this wrong use of our tongue. Try to stop gossiping and controlling what you say on your own, and almost certainly you will fail. See the outstretched nail-pierced hands of Jesus before you beckoning. He cares because He is the truth and wants to establish what He is within you.

The good life is never intended to be a constant rallying of self-effort, but a willing submission to all that He wants and a glad surrender to allowing Him to be God in us and then through us.

≈ 11 ≈

A genuinely satisfying life

The Bible is a unique and interesting book for a number of reasons. During World War II 9,500,000 copies of the New Testament were given to members of the armed forces by the Gideons. Hundreds of letters were received back saying how it had given comfort in loneliness; courage where fear invaded the human heart; and hope when despair dominated the dispirited soul. In 1987 after Cory Aquino had her presidency of the Philippines re-affirmed by 80 per cent of the population of that nation for a period of six years, General Fidel Ramos issued every Filipino soldier with a copy of the New Testament which was to be carried in the top right-hand pocket of his battle tunic. 'Back to the Bible' notes on the contents of the Bible were issued to be carried in the top left-hand pocket of his battle tunic.

Poetry has often fed on it. The verses of men like Dylan Thomas and T. S. Eliot are steeped in its idiom. The verbal images of a man like author John Osborne are strongly conditioned by it. Its contemporary influence is immense.

In 1963 Dr Billy Graham, the well-known evangelist who has reached millions with the Gospel of Christ – more than any other human being at any other time in history – says,

> 'One day some years ago I decided to accept the Scriptures by faith ... When I accepted the Scriptures as the authoritative word of God – by faith – I found immediately that it became a flame of fire in my hands. That flame

began to melt away unbelief in the hearts of many people and to move them to decide for Christ. The Word became a hammer, breaking up strong hearts and shaping them into the likeness of God'.

There are two unmistakable things which the Bible does. First of all, it gives an analysis of the human predicament. Secondly, it gives an answer to the human predicament. In other words, whatever version of this book you use it will always speak to our human condition. It will not provide an economic blueprint for a nation nor will it promise a Utopia on the basis of some political philosophy. It will not even offer a facile formula for social betterment. But it does realistically offer an abundant, exuberant, liberating life in Jesus.

When I was struggling personally with my own spiritual life during my undergraduate days at Glasgow University I discovered to my great surprise – for I had been reared in a strongly Christian home where the Bible was revered – that the attraction and vindication of the Bible for me was not so much what it said about God, but what it said about man. I concluded in my confusion and unhappiness that if one was true then I could with honesty and integrity assume that the other was too! Such was the nature and foundation of my personal return to a functioning and firm belief in God, and in His Son Jesus Christ. In the Bible man after man and woman after woman were ruined by this one thing – a desire for something which did not belong to them and which they ought not to have anyway.

In the Old Testament – at the beginning of it all – Eve saw something which she did not have; wondered why she could not have it; and wanted it. Lot, the nephew of Abraham, looked at the Promised Land with his uncle. He was offered a choice of location and land which he would be able to possess. He saw the Jordan valley which was fertile and attractive and seemed to offer unlimited prosperity and well-being. He chose that and went to live in a place called Sodom which was next door to Gomorrah. Achan heard, with everyone else in the army of God, that looting from the enemy was forbidden, and could not understand why he could not benefit from the spoils of war. He desired and so he took, and as a result brought a whole nation to the brink of disaster and ridiculous humiliation. The sons of the priest Eli wrecked their father's ministry and forfeited their own because of their greedy desires which expressed themselves e'erlong. Israel's greatest king, David, saw a pretty woman bathing, and although he knew she was married to one of his most trusted and gallant officers he allowed his desire for her to scramble his honour, integrity and judgment. As a result adultery was committed, murder was ordered, lies were told, a child was born and hearts were broken. Ahab, who appeared not only to have everything he needed, but seemed to have everything he wanted, could not let it rest there. A vineyard belonging to his neighbour Naboth tantalised him. Was it because of what it offered, or was it because it belonged to his neighbour that he could not control his desire to possess it? He procured it – after all, could he not have what he wanted? – and disaster for him resulted.

All of these incidents, and many more in the Old Testament, demonstrate one of the strongest laws of human nature – the more we have, the more we want. It is an unusual, irrational, destructive thing when you think about it, but in one way or another all of us at some time in our lives have known the imperious overbearing demands of this law. In our hearts we say, 'If only I had that; if only I could reach that goal; if only I could become like or behave like so-and-so I would at last be happy and satisfied'.

The New Testament yields its own crop of covetousness. For reasons which are not absolutely clear Judas sold Jesus for 30 pieces of silver – the price of a slave. On the face of it, it was a ridiculous transaction in view of his experience and response to Jesus over three years. In fact he didn't sell his Saviour for that, he sold himself. He did not make a slave out of Jesus, but he made a slave out of himself. Maybe other forces ran high in Judas' soul, but undoubtedly greed was a powerful force that drove him to that treacherous act. In the thrilling record of the growing infant church, Simon Magus saw the power of God being demonstrated through human beings and saw a new means for impressing people and increasing his bank balance. He wanted this reality for the wrong reasons and so he was damned and gave a new word to the English language – simony. In that same romantic story of the early church – even earlier than Simon Magus – Ananias and Sapphira were powerfully attracted to the gracious and generous Barnabas – and wanted the reputation that he so obviously had. They wanted to be thought good church members and practised hypocrisy in order to achieve what they desired. Towards the end of the Acts story the Governor Felix saw Paul as a source of making money – and so tried to build some kind of relationship with the apostle in order that money would change hands – from Paul's to his. That same Paul spoke of one of his companions, Demas, with great sadness. 'Demas has forsaken me', he writes, 'He loved the good things of this life and went to Thessalonica.'

These and many other instances of covetousness tumble out of the pages of the New Testament. The Bible so clearly exposes our human nature. God is never in any doubt of what He is up against when He has to deal with us. The consumer craze of the Western world has appealed powerfully in its offers and marketing to a reality within us which obscures our judgment and often clouds our reason. We argue so cogently, 'I have to maintain my standard of living' – do you? I can remember sitting at lunch with one of our missionaries returned from initiating a written language, translating the Bible into that language, and planning a literacy programme in the Amazonian jungle. 'What changes strike you now that you are back in England?' I asked him. He replied, 'Here you have everything, and yet you have nothing. The Indians have nothing and yet they have everything.' He was impressed by the pressure of the consuming desire for things which so drives our Western society. I daresay that the Indians had their own struggles with covetousness, but it didn't present itself in such a raw and sophisticated way as it does within our society.

There are two main problems associated with the Tenth Commandment. The first problem is that to break it creates great inequality. We want so much more than we already have whilst others have so much less than we already have. This commandment – as others – is addressed in the singular. It has to do with my personal attitude and relationship with my neighbour. It is not directly addressed to nations. However, desires for what I have no right to have or to possess are seen in a much starker and more horrible light when the context is national rather than personal. A person in Britain, for example, eats twenty times as much food in a lifetime as an average Indian does. More than one-fifth of Britons are overweight. So while millions die of starvation in developing countries, we, in Britain, spend millions of pounds on slimming pills and low-calorie food – and this quite apart from health farms, health hydros, massage parlours and countless other devices and machines to get our weight down. We live in a world whose population will grow to 6,000 million by the year 2,000 and in which nine-tenths of the increase will take place in the Third World; in which, although some progress has been made in Third World economic growth, public health, life expectancy and literacy, yet still 800 million people are destitute, meaning that almost 40 per cent of the people in the South are only barely surviving. The North, including Eastern Europe, has a quarter of the world's population and four-fifths of its income, while the South, including China, has three billion people – three-quarters of the world's population – but living on one-fifth of the world's income. We live in a world where every two seconds a child dies of hunger and disease.

Inevitably these staggering statistics must cause us to pause in our attitudes to life in general and to our own particular life-style. 'Is there any criterion by which to decide at what level we should choose to live and how much difference we should permit between ourselves and others in our neighbourhood?' asks John Stott. It is a question that all missionaries have to face when they go from an affluent situation to a developing country. The Willowbank Report is helpful on this topic:

> We do not believe that we should 'go native', principally because a foreigner's attempt to do this may not be seen as authentic, but as play-acting. But neither do we think there should be a conspicuous disparity between our life-style and that of the people around us. In between these extremes, we see the possibility of developing a standard of living which expresses the kind of love which cares and shares, and which finds it natural to exchange hospitality with others on a basis of reciprocity, without embarrassment.

Inequality needs to be challenged in a realistic way rather than talked about. President Nyerere applied this challenge to the building of a Tanzanian State in which 'No man is ashamed of his poverty in the light of another's affluence, and no man has to be ashamed of his affluence in the light of another's poverty'.

Often the aid which is given to developing countries is 'tied' – we stipulate that the country receiving the aid must use it to buy products from the country giving the aid. In 1968 the President of the United States bluntly and rather bravely said to his nation, 'Let us remember, the main purpose of America's foreign aid is not to help other nations, but to help ourselves'. And when you hear of Russia sending snow ploughs to Guinea you realise how crazy this system is – maybe sinister rather than crazy.

Affluent nations are acquisitive nations. Elections are won by the promise of more actual money in your pocket; increased prosperity right across the board; and more goods available in the shops so that there is a much wider selection to choose from. We ought to be amongst the most thankful people in the world as a nation – instead we look for more and spawn discontent into the rising generation. The heart of the matter is within the context of the Tenth Commandment. When we consider what we have we tend to look, not to Latin America, Africa or South East Asia, but to the United States of America and so want and ask for more.

The second main problem associated with the Tenth Commandment is its inwardness. The other nine Commandments are about acts and words, and there is an outwardness about them. This one is inward and has to do with thoughts and feelings. From this point of view it lays the hardest task on a man. To control one's actions and words is one thing, but to control one's thoughts and feelings and emotions is another.

It was a breach of this commandment which produced one of the grimmest records in the annals of Jewish history. Jericho was under seige and the order was given that, when the city was captured, everything in it was to be devoted to the Lord for destruction (Josh 6:17). Human beings, young and old, and animals were to be killed and all the silver, gold, bronze and iron vessels were to be given to the Lord's treasury (Josh 6:19–21). No Israelite was to take anything that was in Jericho as part of the spoils of battle.

Jericho was triumphantly captured. Israel rejoiced. The next city to be taken was, by comparison, tiny and of little consequence. Ai should have fallen to the Israelites without any difficulty whatsoever, but the first attack upon it resulted in a total disaster so far as Israel was concerned (Josh 7:2–5). In the humiliation and confusion which resulted, God revealed to the Israeli commander Joshua that this crushing defeat was the result of the disobedience of one of the Israeli soldiers who, in spite of the order which had been given, kept some of the Jericho spoil for himself (Josh 7:6–15).

'It's true', Achan answered, 'I have sinned against the Lord, Israel's God, and this is what I did. Among the things we seized I saw a beautiful Babylonian cloak, about five pounds of silver, and a bar of gold weighing over one pound. I wanted them so much that I took them. You will find them buried inside my tent, with the silver at the bottom' (Josh 7:20, 21). As a punishment Achan and his family were stoned to death. It was Achan's covetousness which brought disaster to his nation and the terrible death of himself and all his family. It was when 'I saw' and 'I wanted' came together that the trouble really started.

When we go over to the New Testament the desire to have remains equally strong. To the apostle Paul the sin of covetousness was the sin of sins; it was the sin which gave birth to every other sin; and the terrible paradox of this commandment was that it spawned the very sin which it forbade. Paul writes:

> Shall we say, then, that the Law itself is sinful? Of course not! But it was the Law that made me know what sin is. If the Law had not said 'Do not desire what belongs to someone else', I would not have known such desire. But by means of that commandment sin found its chance to stir up all kinds of selfish desires in me. Apart from Law, sin is a dead thing. I myself was once alive apart from Law; but when the commandment came, sin sprang to life, and I died. And the commandment which was meant to bring life, in my case brought death. Sin found its chance, and by means of the commandment it deceived me and killed me. So then, the Law itself is holy, and the commandment is holy, right and good . . . (Rom 7:7–12).

It was in and through this very commandment that sin found its opportunity. It was this commandment which awakened the very sin which it sought to suppress. Here Paul is speaking of an experience which is part and parcel of human nature. Whenever a thing is forbidden it becomes desirable. The command not to covet sometimes gives birth to the desire which covets it. What a man must not have becomes the very thing that above all he desires to have.

The classic expression of this is in Augustine's description of his boyhood experience which he includes in his *Confessions*:

> There was a pear tree near our vineyard, laden with fruit. One stormy night we rascally youths set out to rob it and carry our spoils away. We took off a huge load of pears – not to feast upon ourselves, but to throw them to the pigs, though we ate just enough to have the pleasure of forbidden fruit. They were nice pears, but it was not the pears that my wretched soul coveted, for I had plenty better at home. I picked them simply in order to become a thief. The only feast I got was a feast of iniquity, and that I enjoyed to the full. What was it that I loved in that theft? Was it the pleasure of acting against the law, in order that I a prisoner under rules might have a moment's counterfeit of freedom by doing what was forbidden? . . . The desire to steal was awakened simply by the prohibition of stealing. The pears were desirable simply because they were forbidden.

This, in fact, is the pattern of the first of all sins as the Bible records the event (Gen 3:1–7). It is as psychologically true today as it was in the morning of time.

This, then, was the only commandment that Saul of Tarsus failed to keep as a devout Jew. He speaks forthrightly and honestly of himself as being blameless so far as the Law was concerned. The simple reason for this was that whilst he could exercise discipline and control over his actions and his words, no one could see within his heart – and it was there that the battle raged at its fiercest and he lost. In his most honest moments he knew there was a commandment which he really could not keep – the Tenth.

So often our deepest and most powerful problems are unseen and hidden. Winchester Cathedral began to fall into ruins in 1906. On investigation it was discovered that the Norman builders, all these generations ago, had built on a bed of peat. Only a few feet lower down was solid rock, but they had not dug deeply enough. The same situation caused the tower of Peterborough Cathedral to become very dangerous and it had to be rebuilt in 1882. The old builders had stopped short of rock by three inches. The danger and weakness lay hidden where no one could see. All was well for a while, and then what could be seen was in danger of collapse. These two incidents are good parables of life in general. This commandment goes much deeper than what is seen.

Jesus very clearly taught in the Sermon on the Mount (Matt 5–7) that a man is judged by God not only on the deeds that he does, but on the desires that he has. By the world's standards a man is a good man if he never does a forbidden thing. Neither the world nor a court of law is concerned to judge his thoughts. We are able and allowed to think what we like as long as we neither do nor say what is in fact in our minds. By the standards of Jesus, however, a man is not a good man until he never even desires the forbidden thing. Jesus is concerned about a man's thoughts and feelings every bit as much as He is concerned about a man's acts and words.

Three insistent things emerge from all of this. First of all we need to realise the area of conflict where real battles are really fought. It is not what I do or say which is of the greatest importance, but what I am that matters. Paul writing to the struggling church at Corinth says, 'When someone becomes a Christian he becomes a brand new person *inside* . . .' (2 Cor 5:17 in the Living Bible). Secondly, we need to recognise in view of this that God alone has the ability to judge men. God alone can see the secrets of men's hearts. Many a man whose actions are a model of moral rectitude and can stand openly in judgment before men, stands condemned before God because his thoughts and desires are not right. By this criterion his goodness collapses.

Thirdly, we need to rejoice that even though, by this teaching, every one of us is in default, and not one of us can face this judgment with optimism and hope, yet the grace of God is far greater than all our sin – both on the inside as well as on the outside. Even if we lived a life of outward moral perfection there are none who can truthfully say they have never experienced wrong desires for the forbidden thing, yet God who knows our heart just as well as our hands wants to forgive and cleanse and renew.

There are certain pursuits which accentuate the implications of this commandment. *Collecting* is one of these pursuits. Collecting things in itself is not wrong, and in fact can be positively good when its aim is both to preserve what is valuable from the past and to provide for dependants in the future. However, it can carry with it significant temptation when desiring something which does not belong to you becomes an issue. There are two questions which the collector needs to ask. First of all he needs to ask, 'What is my collection doing to me? Is it making me proud and greedy? Am I now motivated by the fact that now I have more or by what I have is better than what anyone else has?' Secondly he needs to ask, 'What will my collection do for someone else? Will it give others pleasure and stimulate them as much as me or is what I have collected purely a selfish indulgence giving pleasure only to me?'

It is so easy to become possessed by our possessions. I remember sleeping one night in a home where the man of the house collected clocks. They were everywhere – all over each room on the walls and mantelpiece and on tables; even the stairway was covered in clocks both standing and hanging. Midnight was bedlam! I discovered later that his regular and expected practice on a Sunday in church was to sleep his way through the sermon. He never pretended otherwise. As soon as the text or subject for the sermon was announced he consciously and obviously settled down to sleep. I suppose it was hardly surprising since sleep was almost impossible in his house of clocks.

Bargaining is another of these pursuits. How easily bargaining can feed greed. I can easily find myself buying something which I neither need nor want because it appeals to my greed to get it at that price. One of my predecessors in a church where I became the pastor left many abiding memories. He certainly was a kindly man with great compassion for people, but his house which eventually became my home was akin to an auction market. If anything was wanted which could no longer be bought and no one any longer used, then often if you applied to the manse it would be found there. He spent hours bargaining at sales and auctions for things which he certainly did not need and often which others did not want. I don't think the church benefited greatly from his obsession.

Yet another pursuit which comes into conflict with this commandment is *gambling*. Many struggle with the embargo which Christians rightly put on gambling. What is wrong with it? First of all it interferes with faith. A gamble is a transaction between two parties whereby the transfer of something of value is made dependent on chance in such a way that the whole gain of one party equals the whole loss of the other. The essential element is the determination of ownership by an appeal to chance. In gambling chance or luck is the chief element.

The Christian acknowledges that the God he worships governs the universe and rules in the affairs of men. With God nothing is left to chance – and it is this fact which gives confidence and assurance to those who put their trust in Him. In view of this it is inconsistent and irrational for any Christian to appeal to or trust in luck or chance. Gambling is the antithesis of faith and it is an insult to God if we go through life looking for a 'little bit of luck' instead of trusting the One who is in control.

Secondly, gambling has an inherent quality about it which gives it the potential to infect the human personality. Gordon Moody in the *New Statesman* writes that 'Any prolonged examination of gambling reveals a considerable number of habituated gamblers having a great variety of backgrounds and occupations'. He goes on to say, 'Because it is thoughtless it is immoral to dismiss anyone who gambles to excess as either a fool or a knave, when he may be only more vulnerable than the rest'. There certainly has been an increase in those who have become chronic gamblers and the setting up of an organisation called Gamblers Anonymous is a testimony to this.

It is not a new thing, but it can have devastating consequences. I worked for three years as an Assistant Minister in the north of Glasgow in an area which was desperately depressed socially. The two most prevalent issues that confronted most families there were excessive drinking and gambling. Even to this day I can see the pain in the eyes of the gambler and his dependants as they struggled with this issue in practical daily living. For all of them it began simply and in what would be regarded as an innocent way.

Thirdly, gambling undoubtedly inflames the acquisitive spirit—and that is what the Tenth Commandment is all about. No one would question that gambling is patently about getting rather than giving. Commenting on the national spirit in Britain of getting (what's in it for me?) rather than giving in the light of the fact that gambling is one of our boom industries, Dr William Lillie says, 'Each gambling individual is doing his part to perpetuate and aggravate this unhappy economic condition'. Gambling certainly panders to the greed in man's heart. It is blatantly concerned to get something for nothing or for as little as possible. It inflames a desire to get rich quickly with little or no effort at all.

God has given this commandment not because He is capricious nor because He makes arbitrary judgments. In *Snowwhite and the Seven Dwarfs*, on the discovery of Snowwhite the conversation goes like this:

> 'What is it?' they asked.
> 'A woman' snaps Grumpy. 'I don't like them'.
> 'Why not?' questions Doc.
> 'They're full of wicked wiles' returns Grumpy.
> 'What are wicked wiles?' asks Sleepy.
> 'I don't know, but I'm against them,' replies Grumpy.

To many, God is like this—He is against anything, everybody and everything which seems to bring pleasure and enjoyment. There seems to be no reason for His prohibitions or opposition other than to stop us doing things that seem to be pleasurable. However, nothing could be further from the truth. God calls a thing a sin because it is bad for us. Not only is He God and so is wiser than we are, but He is also our Creator and He made us and presumably He knows what is good for us. God knows what greed will do to a person in the long term – it will destroy him.

Experience alone tells us that greed brings great dissatisfaction along with it. The more a man has the more he wants. Satisfaction eludes him once he is set on this course. He becomes obsessed with wants rather than needs. God is concerned in a variety of ways to assure us and remind us that He has always been concerned to deal with our needs. He is our Father and so He wants to be our provider at every level of our personality – materially, mentally, morally, spiritually, emotionally and physically. This is the remarkable good news that we preach.

Again, greed is inherently deceptive. It deceives us in two quite fundamental ways. First of all we can be so easily deceived into thinking that we are successful if we possess a lot. Many times through the years parents have said to me about their children, 'He really has done very well for himself'. Normally that means that he now has position and possessions. The criterion for doing well in the society in which we live is that the more you have the more successful you are judged to be. We are easily convinced that 'A man's life consists in the abundance of things he possesses'. In fact the truth is that 'A man's life consists in the nature of the things which possess him'.

Secondly, we can be easily deceived into thinking that the more we have, the more secure we will be. Jesus tells a devastating story (Luke 12:13–21) of a man who fell for that. He remembered the wrong things. For example he was obsessed with himself. It has been pointed out that there never was a soliloquy so full of the first person singular as the soliloquy of this rich fool. He thought within himself; he talked the matter over, held a dialogue and discussion with himself. It seems that, so far as he was concerned, no one else really existed at all. Secondly, he remembered this world – in fact he appeared never to have had a thought for anything except the world in which he was living. The idea of such a person is to get and get and get things which, he believes, can buy and ensure happiness and security. There is an unwritten saying of Jesus, one of these sayings which were not written down in any Gospel, but which came down from mouth to mouth – 'The world is a bridge. The wise man will pass over it, but will not build his house upon it.' He meant that the world is of first-rate importance, but that it is a stage to another world, and that he who forgets that has really forgotten the main aim and object of life. After all this world is the land of the dying, for people die in this world, but we are travelling to the land of the living where death is no more.

Not only did the man remember and emphasise the wrong things, but he forgot the essential things. He forgot his neighbours. If his barns were too small to hold his bumper crop there must have been many who would have been only too glad to have shared in his surplus, for these were the days before butter mountains and milk lakes. It is certain that if he had only looked around him he could have found many a way of disposing of the excess that he had. One of the gravest and greatest tests of man is – where does he look for and find his enjoyment? Does he connect enjoyment entirely with himself? Or does he connect enjoyment with making other people happy? If he seeks joy in solely selfish enjoyment he will not get it. Barrie summed it up, 'Those who bring sunshine into the lives of others cannot keep it from their own'.

The man also forgot time. The whole attitude of this man was that he had all the time in the world; it never occurred to him that time could possibly have a limit or an end. It is one of the consistent features of all great men that they have been impressed, sometimes obsessed, with the shortness of time. C. E. Montague tells how he first realised the shortness of time. He heard a sermon from Jowett, the Master of Baliol. In it Jowett said, 'I find it set down in tables that the average duration of human life at the age of 21 is 36 years. We may hope for a little more; we may fear a little less, but speaking generally 36 years of about 13,000 days is the term in which our task must be accomplished'. It was the reduction of the matter to days which struck Montague; and there came to him the utter certainty that not one of those days could be wasted by any honourable man. It may well be said that the most dangerous word in the English language is the word 'tomorrow'. It may be a grim thought, but it is a necessary thought, that we have no bond on time. There is no one who knows if for him tomorrow will ever come. The rich fool forgot time. It is told of Alexander the Great that at every feast and occasion of joy he kept a little model of a skeleton on the table beside him to remind him that, even at its happiest, time was short and death must come.

Thirdly, the man forgot God. The proverb says, 'Man proposes; but God disposes'. In the very practical little letter of James, the writer says, 'Now listen to me, you that say "Today or tomorrow we will travel to a certain city, where we will stay a year and go into business and make a lot of money." You don't even know what your life tomorrow will be! You are like a puff of smoke, which appears for a moment and then disappears. What you should say is this: "If the Lord is willing we will live and do this or that"' (Jas 4:13, 14). The man who makes all his plans and then leaves God out has surely left out the most important factor of all.

Finally, he forgot that a man is what he is and not what he has. The rich fool concentrated everything on the pursuit of the things that he was bound to leave behind him and forgot completely the things he could take with him.

The supreme aim of life should not be the acquisition of temporary things, but the formation of a self and a character which some day we may take without shame to God. If we aim at that and with the enabling grace of God go some way to achieving it, then we shall meet the demand of the parable because we shall then be rich in God's sight even though we may be poor in man's.

Greed, then, deceives us about the nature of success and the reality of security. Greed also brings destruction with it. Again in a powerful teaching (Matt 13:1–23) Jesus speaks about His word being like living seed with all the potential for growth and fruitfulness. But 'the worries about this life and the love for riches' are like those bushes which choke the seed which could have brought life and liberty, fulfilment and fruitfulness.

So God laid it down that this Tenth Commandment was to be observed to protect and preserve us from a very strong drive in our nature which will never bring ultimate satisfaction, and it has within it strong tendencies to deceive us and beguile us. If left unbridled and uncontrolled our desire to possess what does not belong to us will destroy what is good and wholesome and creative and fulfilling.

How best can we react and respond to this commandment? First of all by getting into a right relationshp with God. I am not here speaking of making a decision for Christ or subscribing to a creed no matter how accurate and honourable it may be. Nor am I speaking of joining a church of one denomination or none. Nor am I speaking about being baptised after the fashion of the New Testament or responding to the inestimable privilege and joy of 'feeding on Christ by faith with thanksgiving in our hearts'. I am speaking of the spiritual miracle that occurs when we realise that 'God's divine power has given us everything we need to live a truly religious life through our knowledge of the one who called us to share in his own glory and goodness. In this way He has given us the very great and precious gifts He promised, so that by means of these gifts you may escape from the destructive lust that is in the world, and may come to share the divine nature'. I am speaking of discovering what it really means to be a son of God and a living, secure member of God's family.

The reality of being a Christian is so absolutely overwhelming that we can only say with breathless wonder:

> Were the whole realm of nature mine,
> That were an offering far too small.
> Love, so amazing, so divine;
> Demands my soul, my life, my all.

Long ago in our own land in more primitive times a missionary of Christ who came to these shores was asked about Christianity, and he described it as 'Wonder upon wonder; and every wonder true'.

Such is the intense pull of our human nature and the severe struggle that the Tenth Commandment initiates that nothing less than this reality of a right and real relationship with God will suffice.

Following hard on from that will be not only securing a right relationship with God, but also giving a right response to God. Juan Carlos Ortiz says:

> When a man finds Jesus, it costs him everything. Jesus has happiness, joy, peace, healing, security, eternity. Man marvels at this pearl and says, 'I want this pearl. How much does it cost?'
>
> The seller says, 'It's too dear, too costly.'
>
> 'But how much?'
>
> 'Well, it's very expensive.'
>
> 'Do you think I could buy it?'
>
> 'Oh, of course. Anybody can.'
>
> 'But you say it is too expensive. How much is it?'
>
> 'It costs everything you have – no more, no less – so anybody can buy it.'
>
> 'I'll buy it.'
>
> 'What do you have? Let's write it down.'
>
> 'I have $10,000 in the bank.'
>
> 'Good, $10,000. What else?'
>
> 'I have nothing more. That's all I have.'
>
> 'Have you nothing more?'
>
> 'Well, I have some dollars here in my pocket.'
>
> 'How many?'

'I'll see: 30, 40, 50, 80, 100, 120 – 120 dollars.'

'That's fine. What else do you have?'

'I have nothing else. That's all.'

'Where do you live?'

'I live in my house.'

'The house too.'

'Then you mean I must live in the garage?'

'Have you a garage, too? That too. What else?'

'Do you mean that I must live in my car?'

'Have you a car?'

'I have two.'

'Both become mine. Both cars. What else?'

'Well, you have the house, the garage, the cars, the money, everything.'

'What else?'

'I have nothing else.'

'Are you alone in the world?'

'No, I have a wife, two children . . .'

'Your wife and your children too.'

'Too?'

'Yes, everything you have. What else?'

'I have nothing else. I am left alone now.'

'Oh, you too. Everything. Everything becomes mine! Wife, children, house, garage, cars, money, clothing, everything. And you too. Now you can use all these things here, but don't forget they are mine, as you are. When I need any of the things you are using you must give them to me because now I am the owner.'

No other response will adequately lick our complete inability to face up to the challenging implications of the Tenth Commandment. No other response adequately understands the practical implication of confessing that 'Jesus Christ is Lord.' How often we have presented and absorbed a cheap and superficial Gospel and wondered in our heart of hearts why it did not work properly.

We are so built and constructed that we must desire

something; and we need to come to terms with the fact that these instinctive desires we have are the strongest part of our nature. They constitute a powerful, dynamic, driving power within us. The value of any powerful force depends entirely on the use that is made of it. Nuclear power, for example, can provide power to drive machines, bring light to communities and make life much easier for all the world, but that same nuclear power can be used, and has been used, to bring destruction and death throughout the world, so that by its use mankind could commit genocide. Alongside this we need to be aware constantly that the way any power is used will depend on the character and heart of the man who possesses it. If nuclear power is in the hands of those who only want to benefit and help mankind, then, of course, it can be a very great blessing. If it is in the hands of those who are consumed by personal, national, or racial ambitions, it can ruin mankind.

In a real sense this is a perfect analogy of the nature of man. Man's desires will drive him to long for things, and to take such action as he can to get them. If he is driven by selfish ambition and by the desire to get, then the desire will issue in a covetousness which cannot be other than an evil thing. If, however, there is in his heart a love for God and a love for man which is being supernaturally planted and rooted there by the Holy Spirit, then he will only want the best gifts that will bless God and benefit man. His desire, his covetousness, his driving power will be for the things that are high and holy and good and true and lovely.

Desire cannot be eradicated from the heart of man. Man will always covet something. It is only when Jesus Christ reigns in reality in his heart that the desire for the wrong will be eradicated and the desire for the good will become the dynamic of his life.

This is the good life. The appeal to want the good life is quite legitimate, but the way to find it and experience it has often been confused. You cannot buy the good life—no matter how much money you have and spend. We live in a society which has more appliances, facilities, gadgets and pleasing designs than our society at any other time. And yet we struggle as a nation with more anxieties, worries and fears, to say nothing of boredom, than we have ever known in our history. What has gone wrong?

With unflinching intensity and simplicity the Bible declares that the good life is something which money cannot buy. The really good life can only and exclusively be enjoyed by people who are morally and spiritually disciplined. God's way to the good life is no secret. He has given us ten steps to good living in the ageless and indispensable Ten Commandments. This is His way to the good life.